FORUM FOR SOCIAL STUDIES (FSS)

FSS Studies on Poverty No. 1

Some Aspects of Poverty in Ethiopia:

Three Selected Papers

Edited by
Dessalegn Rahmato
Forum for Social Studies (FSS)

Addis Ababa
Forum for Social Studies
March 2003

ISBN: 1-904855-69-5
ISBN-13: 978-1-904855-69-9

Layout by: Mihret Demissew

Table of Contents

Tables

Acronyms

ADLI	Agricultural-Development-Led-Industrialization
AIDS	Acquired Immune Deficiency Virus
CADU	Chilallo Agricultural Development Unit
CBOs	Community-based Organizations
CBDSD	Capacity Building for Decentralized Service Delivery
CSA	Central Statistical Authority
DHS	Demographic and Health Survey
DHS	Demographic and Housing Survey
EEA	Ethiopian Economic Association
DPPC	Disaster Prevention and Preparedness Commission
FAO	Food and Agriculture Organization
FDRE	Federal Democratic Republic of Ethiopia
GDP	Gross Domestic Product
GNP	Gross National Product
GOE	Government of Ethiopia
HA	Hectares
HAMCO	HIV/AIDS Mitigation and Control Office
HICE	Household Income and Consumption Expenditure
HIV	Human Immunodeficiency Virus
ICRW	International Center for Research on Women
IDP	Internally Displaced People
IDS	Institute of Development Studies (University of Sussex)
IEC	Information, Education and Communication
KG	Kilogram
MEDaC	Ministry of Economic Development and Cooperation currently known as MoFED
MHRC	Miz-Hasab Research Center
MoFED	Ministry of Finance and Economic Development
MOH	Ministry of Health
MOLSA	Ministry of Labor and Social Affairs
MT	Metric Tons
NAC	National AIDS Council
NGOs	Non-Governmental Organizations
PLWHA	People Living With HIV/AIDS
PRSP	Poverty Reduction Strategy Paper
Qn	Quintal
RRC	Relief and Rehabilitation Commission
SC-UK	Save the Children – U.K.
SSA	Sub-Saharan Africa
TB	Tuberculosis
TGE	Transitional Government of Ethiopia
UDAs	Urban Dwellers Associations
UMP	Urban Management Program
UNAIDS	Joint United Nations Program on HIV/AIDS
UNCHS	United Nations Center for Human Settlements
UNDP	United Nations Development Program
UNICEF	United Nations Children's Fund
WADU	Wollaita Agricultural Development Unit
WMU	Welfare Monitoring Unit

Introduction

The three papers published in this volume were originally presented at the First International Conference on the Ethiopian Economy held here in Addis Ababa on 3-5 January 2003 and organized by the Ethiopian Economic Association (EEA). The conference, which attracted a large audience, including a number of Ethiopians from the Diaspora community, heard over seventy papers and oral presentations delivered by academics, researchers, public servants and professionals from a wide diversity of institutions and backgrounds. Following the request of EEA, FSS hosted a special panel on poverty at the Conference in which the three papers and an oral presentation by Prof. Bahru were delivered for discussion. Prof. Bahru's presentation, which was warmly received by the audience, was on poverty in historical perspective but unfortunately, due to the pressure of work, he has been unable to prepare a paper for publication.

FSS has identified poverty as one of its priorities areas around which it has undertaken a broad set of activities including research and publication, policy debates, advocacy work and public awareness programs. Its Poverty Dialogue Forum, an extended program which run from the end of 2000 to the middle of 2002, provided an open forum for wide ranging public discussions on the nature of poverty in this country and what must be done to address it following the government's poverty reduction strategy paper (PRSP) initiative. One of the end results of this program was a series of seven publications in which concerned individuals from civil society organizations, the private sector, government agencies, donor organizations, academics and the poor themselves discuss poverty and poverty reduction from their own particular perspectives. This special publication is part of FSS on-going concern about poverty and we hope to present other discussions on the subject in this or other format in the future.

1

Poverty and Agricultural Involution

Dessalegn Rahmato

Introduction

In February 1997, Prime Meles Zenawi delivered his annual report to Parliament in which he triumphantly declared that thanks to the success of the new agriculture package and extension program, the country had finally achieved food self-sufficiency. The harvest of the last two years, he said, was the best in the country's history, and henceforth Ethiopia will free itself from the scourge of hunger and starvation that had plagued the rural people for countless generations. He attributed this unprecedented achievement to the sound economic policies of his government, and in particular to the agricultural development strategy it had pursued since the middle of the 1990s[1]. Some five weeks after this jubilant speech, DPPC announced that several million peasant farmers in various parts of the country were facing severe food shortages and made an urgent appeal to the donor community for food aid. It was obvious that the Prime Minister had a poor grasp of the conditions of Ethiopian agriculture, and mistook what was in effect the feeble squeak of a moribund economy as the joyous song of its rebirth.

Every year in January, the Ethiopian government summons all donor agencies in the capital and reports to them how many people will be facing starvation in the year ahead and how much food aid will be urgently needed to avert a catastrophe. This grim ritual has been performed regularly since the late 1970s. Every year the number of people at risk, and hence the volume of emergency assistance requested, increases. Figures from RRC/DPPC, the government's disaster management agency, show that between 1980 and 1989, the vulnerable population averaged 4.2 million annually; between 1992 and 2001, the average was 5.3 million. A joint Government - UN appeal issued in December 2002 reports that 21 percent of the population (or over 14 million people) are estimated to be at risk, of which 11.3 million require immediate emergency assistance. It is expected that about one and half million metric tons of food aid will be necessary to avert a colossal tragedy. There are now millions of rural people who have become dependent on food aid for over a decade and half.

Famine has been a recurrent tragedy in Ethiopia during much of the twentieth century, bringing death and suffering to millions of people, and, helping to undermine the authority of two of the country's recent regimes. The virulent famines of the mid 1960s, 1970s and 1980s, in which innumerable lives were lost, and which became international

---

[1] *Addis Zemen*, 30 Tir 1989 Eth. Cal (7 February 1997). For the full text of the speech see the next four issues of the paper.

media events, are still fresh in many people's minds in the countryside. More recently, the crisis of 1994 and the famine of 1999 provide added evidence that dearth and starvation have structural causes and are not a product of temporary social or environmental shocks. Moreover, behind these landmark tragedies are a number of localized disasters which do not often attract media attention (nor, at times, the attention of the national authorities), but whose impact on the victims has been just as devastating as the more celebrated tragedies. We know from the available evidence that previous centuries were not free from famine, nevertheless it does appear (though the evidence is at present patchy) that the frequency of famine in the country has become much greater and its impact much more devastating in the second half of the twentieth century (see Dessalegn 1994). Famine is deeply embedded in peasant consciousness: it shapes farmers' livelihood strategies and social relationships, conditions their attitude to the land and the environment, and regulates the rhythm of production and consumption. While at one level peasants may attribute famine to Divine intervention or Fate, at another level they recognize that it is the poor and the destitute that suffer from its impact.

The evidence is compelling that over the last fifty years rural poverty has been growing in severity and magnitude on the one hand, and that the country's agriculture has been in structural decline on the other. This is confirmed not just by recurrent incidents of mass starvation, which by itself is sufficient to prove our point, but also by high rates of morbidity and mortality, excessive levels of asset depletion, and, in general, increasing livelihood vulnerability among farming households. Poverty and agricultural decline are closely inter-related, forming a dynamic process in which the one helps to reinforce the other. This process must be seen against a background of frequent civil wars and communal conflicts inflicting a heavy toll on rural society, and predatory governance and institutional instability.

The aim of this paper is to take a critical look at the causes of deepening poverty and agricultural decline, and in particular to examine what I call the structural shifts that have occurred over the half-century since the 1950s and have been responsible for peasant misfortune and economic malaise. Due to space limitations, I shall not review the agricultural history of the country in the period in question, though I do realize that such a review would have yielded valuable insights about the forces that shaped the changes that I am concerned about. There is virtually no serious work on agricultural history covering the modern period of the country, though McCann (1987, 1995) may be cited as the exception even if his time horizon does not frequently extend beyond the early decades of the twentieth century. My own attempt to review the history of agricultural policy during the Imperial period is brief and incomplete (Dessalegn 1995). What I shall set out to do is not so much provide new findings and fresh empirical data as suggest broad frameworks for analyzing the data that is already available, and in so doing hope to stimulate debate on the subject at hand and on the development challenges facing the rural economy. What is lacking and urgently needed in this country is a sustained analytical debate on the economy in general and on agrarian change in particular.

I shall set my discussion in the framework of two broad and closely linked arguments. First, I submit that most rural households are experiencing an erosion of their livelihood capabilities, none more seriously than the poor, a considerable number of whom are falling into the ranks of the destitute. This *downward* mobility in general, and the shift from poverty to destitution in particular has been going on for some time but has not been sufficiently examined in the existing literature[2]. Second, Ethiopian agriculture has been undergoing what I wish to call a *process of involution* since the second half of the twentieth century. As I shall try to show further down, the concept of agricultural involution is not synonymous with agricultural decline but has a broader meaning and significance (vid. Geertz 1963).

From Poverty to Destitution

The distinction between poverty and destitution and the boundary between one and the other is difficult to determine with any degree of precision, nevertheless it is a valid distinction to make and is frequently employed by peasants themselves who use a range of criteria (and a rich vocabulary)[3] to distinguish between those who are poor and those who are destitute. Some of the criteria for determining poverty or destitution commonly employed in rural communities include the following: a) Live assets: these consist of farm oxen, other livestock, and household labor. b) Property, which often means agricultural land, though it may include housing or property in nearby towns. c) Cash income derived either from on-farm or off-farm activities, as well as remittances. d) A combination of any or all of the above. In each particular case, there is a commonly agreed upon cut-off point which separates one category of peasants (the destitute) from another (the non-destitute). Such measures may present difficulties to those who may wish to construct statistical aggregates or a numerical picture of destitution because the cut-off points may appear to be arbitrarily determined, or vary from one community to another. Thus if in one community a destitute is one who has only one sheep or goat, in another he/she may be defined as someone who owns no livestock at all. Despite this drawback, peasant measurements of destitution are empirically sound because they are based on what communities consider critical assets for rural livelihood. The approach taken by MEDAC/MOFED to define poverty on the basis of a minimum level of consumption goods is not radically different from the peasant approach and may be faulted on similar grounds. I have argued elsewhere that since the land reform of the 1970s, live assets, in particular farm oxen and labor power, are the most appropriate factors determining well-being or deprivation among rural households (Dessalegn 1997). In all three cases, the emphasis is on economic goods, and thus both may be described as "economist" approaches to destitution.

A different attempt to define destitution from a broader perspective appears in a recent policy study conducted in Wollo (north and south) and Wag Hamra by IDS for Save the Children-U.K (2002). This study is one of the few works in this country to examine destitution and to try to measure its magnitude in a rural setting. The report adopts a modified version of the "sustainable livelihoods" approach and defines destitution as a "state of extreme poverty that results from the pursuit of 'unsustainable livelihoods'". Individuals in this condition are said to be unable to meet their subsistence needs, have

---

[2] For a brief review of the Ethiopian poverty literature, see Aklilu and Dessalegn (2000)
[3] See Aklilu and Dessalegn 2000, and IDS 2002 for the local vocabulary of destitution

inadequate access to productive resources, and are dependent on assistance from others (: 9). Since the aim of the study was to raise the awareness of policy makers about destitution and chronic food insecurity and to help identify feasible policies to address these problems, there is greater emphasis placed on measurable indicators.

I shall view poverty and destitution within a broadly conceived livelihood framework but I shall place more emphasis on a different set of factors, which, unfortunately for some, do not often lend themselves to precise measurement. Poverty and destitution are both states of *livelihood deprivation* but differing in degree. Both involve the erosion of a household's productive, purchasing and bargaining power on the one hand, and its social and institutional resources on the other. Destitution is an extreme form of deprivation. In this definition, poverty or destitution is seen both as a condition as well as a relationship, an end result as well as a process. In most cases, destitution is a downward slide from poverty- i.e., the destitute are those who were once poor but now find themselves in conditions of extreme deprivation due to the further erosion of their livelihood capabilities and resources. There are of course exceptions to this rule: those, for example, born into destitution (the siblings of the destitute), and, on rare occasions, well-to-do households that have been thrown into destitution by extraordinary circumstances are two cases in point.

The IDS study found that 14 percent of the rural population in the study area is destitute. The figure was arrived at by combining a number of single self-assessment indicators and a composite destitution index constructed by the authors. I would argue that this is a low figure for the area and provides a partial picture of the state of rural deprivation. I say this because Wollo and Wag Hamra are one of the poorest areas in the country and have repeatedly been devastated by virulent famine for at least the last fifty years. Acute forms of food insecurity are a regular part of rural life here, and ecological vulnerability continues to severely depress crop and livestock production. There is enormous population pressure on the land and household farm plots are small have been getting smaller over time. Be that as it may, the study looked at trends in destitution and concludes that the incidence of destitution has increased dramatically in the 1990s and that in addition the number of households who were 'doing well' has similarly decreased. This corresponds to the findings of earlier studies which showed an upward trend in poverty and a downward trend in well-being (Aklilu and Dessalegn 2000). The study further identifies the destitute to be female-headed households, older male households, and households which have fewer or no labor power.

I submit that while there are no accurate figures for destitution on a national scale, a strong case can be made for the argument that at present the destitute constitute no less than a third of the rural household population. However, considerable problems emerge when one attempts to examine the transition to destitution over a long timeframe. Determining destitution over a period of half a century, which is what we are attempting to do here, is different from measuring it within a narrow and specific timeframe. It should be borne in mind that we have no benchmark studies that we can use for comparative purposes. My purpose in this discussion is thus to offer a schematic glimpse of the transition from poverty to destitution based on the available evidence. In what follows I shall look at a selected number of factors defining deprivation that I believe can serve as proxy indicators of growing destitution.

First is the frequency of mass starvation. I distinguish between what I call virulent famines on the one hand and hidden famines on the other. Virulent famines involve widespread starvation accompanied by high levels of crisis or excess mortality. The famines of 1957/58, 1964-66, 1973/74, 1984/85, and 1999/2000 fall in this category. Over 150,000 people are reported to have perished in the famine of 1973/74, while the death toll ten years later is estimated to be over 400,000. Hidden famines on the other hand are localized events in which mortality is "hidden" because it occurs over a longer period of time and appears as "backstage" mortality, sometimes reflected in the annual statistics. The crises of the mid-1950s, of 1989/90, and 1994 may be considered "hidden famines" (see Dessalegn 1994 for the chronology famine). Famines, whether virulent or hidden, are accompanied not only by suffering and high mortality, but also by social dysfunction, and a temporary collapse of the local economy. Moreover, even a minor food crisis sets in train a process of asset depletion at the household and community level that may take a long time to reverse. Virulent famine involves a massive loss of "live assets" (labor and livestock), of environmental resources, and household investments. The frequent occurrence of mass starvation aggravates the erosion of household assets and social resources, making it an unremitting process with little chance of recovery. Thus households and communities become progressively impoverished and increasingly vulnerable, making them easy victims to even a minor crisis. The link between famine and destitution is thus a direct one, and from a historical perspective famine must rank as the most important causal factor for the transition from poverty to destitution in this country. In Wollo and the northeast, there are many rural households who were thrown into abject poverty by the famine of the mid-1980s and who have not recovered up to now.

The second defining factor of deprivation is reflected in declining food consumption over time. A study prepared in the last years of the 1980s argues that rural cereal consumption has declined in the period 1966/67 to 1982/83 (Watt 1988). Watt found that a comparison of average rural cereal consumption with average national consumption shows that rural consumption has fallen in this period relative to the national average. Moreover, the average consumption of the rural producer has fallen in comparison with that of the urban dweller. According to Watt, mean rural consumption per capita was 138 kg in 1966/67, 110 in 1976/77, 127 in 1979/80, and 95 in 1982/83. While Watt's figures may be subject to debate, his basic argument of continuing declines in rural food consumption cannot be dismissed. There is evidence, though far from robust, that rural food consumption has been declining over the years both in absolute terms as well as in relation to urban consumption. The on-going decline in per capita food production that many studies have shown adds further evidence to this conclusion. Marcos (1997) has shown that per capita food production declined steadily in the 1980s and early 1990s, from 174 kg in 1981/82 to 97.4 in 1993/94. Webb et al (1992) point out that per capita cereal production has been declining by an average of 4 kg per year since the early 1960s. The World Bank (1996) is emphatic that per capita cereal production has shown a sharp decline since the 1950s. "As population has grown from 15 million to 55 million today, the production of cereals has dropped, on a per capita basis, by more than 25 percent- from more than 200 kg of cereal per capita in the early 1950s to less than 150 kg by 1992" (: 4).

The flow of food aid into the country in the last three decades is also a good indication of the growing inability of the farm sector to feed the peasant population. Table 1.1 in the Annex at the end of the paper shows the amount of food aid distributed in the country from 1971 to 2000. In the decade of the 1970s, a total of 688,500 metric tons (mt) of food aid were distributed in the country; on the average, this was 76,500 mt. per year. In the 1980s, the total had jumped to 5.1 million mt, and the annual average was 512,400 mt. In the period 1991 to 2000, the total and annual average figures were 8.0 million and 798,800 mt. respectively. Between 20 to 25 percent of the food consumed in the rural areas in the 1990s was made up of food aid. The growing volume of food aid was both in response to large scale famine and food crises, and the growing population of vulnerable households who were unable to feed themselves and were facing the threat of starvation.

The third evidence of extreme deprivation is malnutrition and the health status of adults and children associated with it. Nutritional vulnerability can be caused by a wide range of factors, including insufficient diet, diet lacking in variety and basic nutrients, famine shocks, and past health experience (malnutrition of the mother, for example). Related to this is life expectancy and mortality. The rates of child and infant mortality in rural Ethiopia are the highest in Sub-Saharan Africa. While infant mortality showed some improvement in the 1990s, child mortality worsened in the same period (World Bank 1999). Child and infant mortality reflect a cumulative process and are determined by the health status of the mother, particularly in childhood. Anthropometric measurements provide a good indication of the nutritional status of vulnerable groups such as children. Recent studies undertaken by CSA (2001) and the findings of the DHS indicate that there have been some improvements in child malnutrition and mortality. This may be true, but we cannot take it as evidence of a positive trend in the future but only a temporary dip in the statistics due to favorable circumstances (improvements in the harvest due to good weather conditions, etc). The underlying causes of malnutrition have not changed, and they will continue to exact a heavy toll on the rural population.

Comparison of child malnutrition in Ethiopia with other countries indicates the harsh realities of poverty in the country. UNICEF's annual report on the world's children shows consistently that since the 1980s malnutrition rates among Ethiopian children are among the highest in the world. One indicator of child malnutrition, in particular, which reflects *long-term* nutritional deprivation is *stunting* (low height for age). Since the beginning of the 1980s, stunting among children in Ethiopia has been getting worse and has remained the highest in the world (UNICEF 2000). According to an earlier CSA report (1993), stunting among children in Ethiopia was 60 percent in 1983 but rose to 64 percent in 1992. The World Bank (1999) notes that there was a further rise in 1995/96, bringing the figure to 68 percent. In comparison, UNICEF notes that stunting in Uganda and Kenya in the early 1990s was 38 and 33 percent respectively.

Persistent malnutrition is a strong indicator of severe poverty and destitution. In an agrarian society such we have here, malnutrition has a serious impact on work, productivity and household income and in effect helps to further aggravate deprivation. Malnutrition is the nutritional landscape on which the footprint of recurrent famine is firmly etched. There are two points that I wish to note here that are relevant to the discussion at hand. First, the depth and extent of rural malnutrition is shockingly high by whatever yardstick we wish to measure it. Second, while there may have been some periodic dips in the figures due to fortuitous circumstances, the evidence suggests that over the long term nutritional vulnerability has worsened in all respects. This is consistent with the argument I posed earlier, namely that there has been a continuous shift from poverty to destitution in the period under discussion.

Agricultural Involution

I shall use the term *involution* to mean a retreat inward, shrinkage, declining vigor, and becoming internally complex and entangled as a result. I have borrowed the concept from the noted American anthropologist, Clifford Gertz who used it to describe the complex process of change and decline in Javanese rice culture after independence (Gertz 1963). I have added some modifications to make it relevant to the conditions of Ethiopian agriculture. I shall look at a selected number of indicators of agricultural involution and discuss their consequences.

I shall start with declining agricultural productivity, which in turn is closely tied to farm plot size and tenure security. This is not the place to examine in depth the tenure system in force since the land reform of the 1970s, however, there is now broad agreement among rural development specialists and practitioners that *tenure insecurity*, with all its attendant ills, is widespread among the farm population and that the land system is largely responsible for it. It is also commonly recognized that household farm plots are small and that there is growing land fragmentation. While the empirical evidence is not sufficiently robust, there is local level evidence showing the decline of farm plots over a period of three to four decades. I have used the findings of the studies undertaken by CADU, WADU and the other integrated development programs during the 1960s and early '70s as useful benchmarks. Huffnagel of FAO (1961), the only valuable work on Ethiopian agriculture in the 1950s does not discuss farm size, although it does provide estimates of yield per hectare for a variety of crops. Some papers published by the staff of Alemaya agricultural college in the 1960s include the distribution of farm size in the localities studied. According to Lexander (1968), for instance, average cultivated area in Chilalo, the most coveted area of Arssi, and the focus of CADU programs, was 2.5 ha in the mid-1960s. Average plot size in the same area in 1997/98 was found to be 1.4 ha. (CSA 1998). At present, CSA estimates that the average plot size for the country as a whole is 0.98 ha. The recent land and agricultural survey undertaken by the EEA (2002) reaches a similar conclusion. All this must be seen against a background of increasing population on the land, which has grown from an estimated 15 million in the early 1950s to 34 million in 1980 and 54 million in 2000.

Agricultural productivity in this country means land productivity and is measured by crop yield. The data in Table 1.2 in the Annex is remarkable in that productivity in the two decades for which reliable data is available shows no discernable change. In fact, the figures in the 1990s are slightly lower than those in the 1980s. The highest yield achieved was 12.8 qn per ha in 1982/83 and 12.5 qn per ha in 1988/89, both during the Derg years. These figures have not been equaled in the years under the present government despite the fact that fertilizers and improved seeds have been distributed much more widely since the mid-1990s than at any time before. The best yield performance under the current agricultural strategy of the government was achieved in the 1996/97 harvest when crop yield reached 11.7 qn per ha. If we combine this with the deterioration of per capita food production noted earlier in this paper, it becomes obvious that the rural economy is increasingly losing its ability to supply a marketable surplus. The evidence thus suggests that peasant agriculture has fallen victim to all the pressures impinging on it and is progressively exhausting its potential.

A second issue that we need to examine here is vulnerability, including ecological vulnerability. The available evidence shows that over the years an increasing number of peasant households have become marginalized, unable to meet their basic needs or even feed themselves. Table 1.3 shows the vulnerable population, on a yearly basis, over the last two decades based on the food requirement figures and needy population issued annually by RRC/DPPC, the government's emergency management agency. In the decades of the 1980s and 1990s, on the average, about 11 percent of the rural population was deemed to be vulnerable and unable to feed itself. In the 1980s, 4.2 million people were vulnerable, in the 1990s, the figure was 5.3 million. Rural marginalization has been made worse by the pressures on peasant agriculture noted above as well as by *growing* landlessness. Moreover, the scarcity of land, population pressure, technological stagnation, the increasing demands of successive governments on an exhausted peasantry, and insufficient market integration have had a further deleterious effect. Over the years, state support to peasant agriculture has been minimal.

Peasant vulnerability must be seen against a background of relentless ecological stress and large-scale degradation of environmental resources. The ecology of involution is evidenced by severe land degradation, in particular the deterioration of soil fertility, the loss of forestry and vegetation cover on a large scale, hillside farming, and the drying up of both surface and sub-surface water. The frequent occurrence of environmental shocks further aggravates ecological vulnerability.

Another factor that is an important element of involution is the absence of social differentiation in rural Ethiopia. The social landscape of the countryside was profoundly altered in the 1970s and '80s by the radical reforms of the Derg, which eliminated the power and property of the landed nobility, local gentry and commercial farmer that, under the Imperial system, dominated the peasant world and exercised a stranglehold on the agrarian economy. Rural Ethiopia has since become a land of small peasants, operating tiny holdings that are losing their viability by the year. Recurrent land redistribution, which was frequent during the Derg and which has been undertaken by the current government as well, has led to the progressive leveling down of household plots, of income and social status. While the government has argued that redistribution and other aspects of the existing land policy have created the opportunity for equality of holdings and thus social equity (MoFED 2002), it is my contention that land policy has spread poverty wider and created equality under poverty. In most rural communities, everyone is poor and getting poorer. This does not mean that there are no differences in livelihood status among rural communities. I have argued elsewhere that in addition to the poor there are what may be termed "middle" and "well-to-do" peasants, using the last two terms in their relative sense (Dessalegn 1997). Others have also noted similar forms of livelihood differentiation among peasant households, but the dominant picture is one of widespread and deep poverty (Yared 2002). Moreover, there is growing evidence that the population of the non-poor is rapidly shrinking as the "better off" are thrown into the ranks of the poor due to the factors noted above (Aklilu and Dessalegn 2000; IDS 2002; Yared 2002). Perhaps it may be useful under the existing conditions to make a distinction between what one may call "livelihood" differentiation and "social" differentiation. The former refers to differences in household or livelihood possessions (someone has a few more goats than another), which are in the main short-lived, while the latter to structural differences that are likely to persist over time.

Differentiation in rural Ethiopia is frequently viewed in terms essentially of asset possession, of labor and income. This is a narrow and inadequate conception of the subject of which I have been one of the guilty ones. Differentiation should also be viewed in terms of product specialization, technology utilization, and the division of labor. The aim of most peasant households is to produce as much of their subsistence as possible, and there is hardly any impetus towards crop or livestock specialization. Moreover, peasants also double up as petty traders, engage in home-produce marketing, and produce many of their own farm and household tools. All these activities have been part of peasant household economy for generations. The rural craftsmen and women are not an important element of rural society in many communities, and in any case, the artisan is an atavistic social force. The main livestock traders are all urban residents.

There have been very limited opportunities for livelihood diversification, with very few avenues for supplementary income either off- or on-farm. A new source of employment, however, which has provided support to needy households has been *food-for-work* which has been widely employed since the famine of the 1970s. During the Imperial regime, large-scale farms in the Awash Valley and the Setit Humera area provided seasonal employment to a considerable number of peasants in the northeast but these farms were subsequently destroyed under the Derg regime.

The division of labor in the countryside is very static and has remained, in the main, unchanged for at least half a century if not more. There is hardly any evidence of demand for new technology, except the use of fertilizers promoted by the government. Trials of new processes of production, or demands for new products are limited and often restricted to farmer training programs or programs undertaken by NGOs. In brief, what we have is a closed economy dependent on its own dwindling resources and decreasing output.

To sum up: agricultural involution is thus much more than declining vigor or deterioration. It also has a profound impact on peasant households, making them turn inward, rather than outward, and concentrate on the immediate demands of subsistence.

9

Peasant economy becomes almost closed to outside influences or initiative, and households lose any need they may have had to look for new products, techniques or labor processes. The risks involved in trying new ideas now become inordinately high and therefore *tradition* becomes the sole anchor in all livelihood pursuits. If there is any investment incurred it is investment on tradition (see Dessalegn 1991). Moreover, under this condition, households are able to sustain their livelihoods only with greater self-exploitation. Self-exploitation here includes intensive and extensive farm labor but bearing only limited fruit, petty but traditional extra-farm activities producing small rewards (the rural version of the informal economy), reducing consumption, and foregoing such needed services such as health care.

Structural Shifts

Agricultural involution over the last half century has also been accompanied by what I call *structural shifts*, and here I shall discuss, briefly, two of those I consider to be the most important.

From smallholder agriculture to micro-agriculture. I submit that there has been a shift from smallholder agriculture to micro-agriculture in the period under discussion. This is a significant shift accompanying the growth of poverty and the stagnation of the rural economy. The shift has been driven in large measure by the land system in place since the second half of the 1970s but whose origins must be sought in the Imperial period. Micro-farm systems are those in which households' basic farm assets (oxen, land, labor, livestock) have become insufficient, and peasants become trapped in production for sheer survival. Such systems cannot support the basic subsistence needs of the family, cannot create assets or reserves, and are highly fragile. They tend to easily collapse under even minimum pressure, such as for example a mild drought, limited rainfall variability, or moderate market fluctuation. Smallholder systems, in contrast, are relatively more resilient than micro-systems. While production for basic subsistence is an important element of smallholder agriculture, households have enough assets to produce some surplus and to create more assets. Precise measures of the relative strength of each system are not currently available, but it is evident that a considerable proportion of rural households are now engaged in micro-farming.

From farm economy to food economy. I shall use the term "food economy" to mean farm activities that are exclusively concerned with food production for own consumption, in which the market plays a marginal role. Cultivators under this system are constrained by a host of factors, some of which noted above, and are unable to go beyond bare subsistence. Cropping strategies consist of selecting those food crops that are critical to the household diet. Thus crop diversification is essentially dependent on the consumption needs of the household. This definition differs from that employed by food economy specialists associated with Save the Children-U.K and other organizations (see, e.g., SC-U.K 1997). A farm economy in contrast is one in which production for consumption progressively becomes secondary and the market assumes a dominant influence. The most mature farm economies are highly specialized and produce exclusively for the market. In between are farm economies in which specialization is emerging and in which the market gradually plays an important role. Some segments of Ethiopian smallholder agriculture were beginning to evolve towards a farm economy in the latter part of the 1960s but this experiment was quashed by the radical reforms of the Revolution in the 1970s (see Dessalegn 1986).

The food economy is highly dependent on the periodic harvest which can mean, for the household, the difference between access to food and starvation. Food economies therefore may be described as *harvest sensitive* economies. The failure of a single harvest has devastating consequences on the household and the local economy, often leading to dearth and starvation. Farmers here cannot turn to the market for their subsistence needs because the harvest defines the local market. Besides, households under this system have little or no access to earned income, except for those who benefit from income transfers from siblings, relatives or friends.

Food economies are essentially dependent economies: they are dependent on food aid, or assistance from outside. Since the harvest is so critical and since, in this country, farming is at the mercy of the vagaries of nature, harvest failures are quite frequent. The millions of peasants who become vulnerable to food shortages each year, shown in Table 1.3, are, in large measure, the victims of harvest failures.

Conclusion

The discussion presented above is in sharp contrast to the existing policy discourse and puts into question the development strategy pursued by the government. The main pillars of the policy discourse are the following: a) Rural centered and agriculture-led development is possible. Agriculture can be the engine of growth and will be able to provide improved living standards, and an increasing flow of raw materials to industry. b) It follows from this that the town should be subordinate to the country, and industry to agriculture. c) Food security can be achieved through food self-sufficiency, which is possible only through growth in local food production. d) Growth in food production will be made possible through the provision, to peasant farmers, of a package of modern inputs of which the main component is chemical fertilizer (FDRE 2001). The policy does not address such critical issues as tenure insecurity, land scarcity and fragmentation of household plots, declining productivity and increasing land degradation. What is also missing from the discourse is a rigorous analysis of poverty and its multifaceted ramifications on rural society.

This is not the place for a critical examination of the policy but a brief comment is in order. We have argued earlier that the process of agricultural decline set in train over four decades ago continues unabated and some of the structural elements of this decline have been examined at some length. Briefly put, Ethiopian agriculture has virtually exhausted its potential and is incapable, in its present form, of serving as the engine of growth and development. The policy discourse does not envisage a structural transformation of the rural sector nor does it open up new opportunities for peasant initiative. Growth and economic improvement is expected to be achieved on the back of micro-farmers, who as we saw above, are threatened with destitution and food insecurity on the one hand, and

11

burdened with insecure holdings, tiny plots, and an undemocratic extension service on the other.

Secondly, the pursuit of food self-sufficiency on the strength of domestic agriculture is highly unrealistic. There are only a handful of countries in the world that are or have the potential to be self -sufficient in food, and all other countries ensure food security for their population through the world market. Indeed, some countries in the Middle East and the Gulf do NOT produce any food at all, and yet there have been no reports of food shortages or widespread hunger in these countries. Increased food output will not mean that each household will have access to adequate food as a matter of course. Access to food depends on one's entitlements and the purchasing power of the family concerned. Opening up employment opportunities for rural households, diversifying their sources of income, and expanding people's capabilities would therefore have been a better alternative.

Annex

Table 1.1: **Cereal Food Aid to Ethiopia 1971-2000 (Thousand Tons)**

The 1970s

Year	Food Aid	Year	Food Aid
1971/72	24.9	76/77	74.7
72/73	1.8	77/78	76.0
73/74	96.1	78/79	162.5
74/75	54.1	79/80	111.5
75/76	86.6		
Average/Year: 76,500		Total Aid: 688,500	

The 1980s

Year	Food Aid	Year	Food Aid
80/81	228.0	85/86	799.2
81/82	189.7	86/87	570.4
82/83	356.4	87/88	823.8
83/84	171.9	88/89	577.8
84/85	868.9	89/90	537.6
Average: 512,400		Total: 5,123,700	

The 1990s*

Year	Food Aid	Year	Food Aid
1991	893.800	1996	297.5
1992	994.2	1997	652.9
1993	652.1	1998	610.4
1994	786.8	1999	1215.2
1995	524.7	2000	1360.6
Average: 798,800		Total: 8,000,000	

Source: FAO 1985, 1986, 1995 (for the years 1971 to 1989/90; date given in crop year).
 * www.fao.org for the years 1991 to 2000. (Date given in calendar year).

Table 1.2: **Area, Production and Yield of Major Crops 1979/80-2000/01**
(Both Seasons)

Year	Area (Mn. Ha.)	Production (Mn. Qn.)	Yield (Qn/Ha)
80/81	5.7	56.6	11.6
81/82	5.7	63.0	11.1
82/83	6.1	78.1	12.8
83/84	5.7	63.4	11.1
84/85	5.9	48.6	8.2
85/86	6.0	54.0	9.0
86/87	5.6	62.6	11.2
87/88	5.9	66.0	11.1
88/89	5.8	71.9	12.5
89/90	5.8	68.5	11.9
Average 80/81-89/90	**5.8**	**64.2**	**11.1**
93/94	7.2	57.4	8.0
94/95	7.7	75.0	9.7
95/96	9.1	103.3	11.4
96/97	8.9	104.4	11.7
97/98	7.7	81.0	10.5
98/99	8.5	88.7	10.4
99/00	8.9	92.3	10.4
2000/01	10.4	110.4	10.6
Average 93/94-00/01	**8.6**	**89.1**	**10.3**

Source: CSO 1987; CSA 1989-2001.

Table 1.3: **Vulnerable Population (Million) 1980-2001**

Year	Rural Pop.	Vulnerable Pop.	% rural Pop.
1980	33.7	3.7	11.0
81	34.8	3.3	9.5
82	35.7	4.2	11.8
83	36.8	4.0	10.9
84	37.9	5.1	13.5
85	39.0	7.9	20.3
86	40.2	6.9	17.2
87	41.3	2.5	6.1
88	42.3	2.1	5.0
89	43.4	2.3	5.3
Average 1980-89	**38.5**	**4.2**	**10.9**
92	44.4	7.6	17.1
93	45.3	5.0	11.0
94	46.2	6.7	14.5
95	47.1	4.0	8.5
96	48.4	2.8	5.8
97	49.8	3.4	6.8
98	51.2	4.3	8.4
99	52.6	5.4	10.3
2000	54.0	7.7	14.3
2001	55.5	6.2	11.2
Average 1992-01	**49.57**	**5.3**	**10.7**

Source: CSA 1991 for population 1980-1989; CSA 1999 for population between 1992-2001; DPPC 1999
  for vulnerable population 1980-1999; DPPC 2000; DPPC 2001.

Note: According to DPPC 1999, vulnerable population in 1991 estimated to be 7.2 million, but since
  this was a transitional year I have left it out.

13

References

Aklilu Kidanu and Dessalegn Rahmato 2000. *Listening to the Poor: A Study Based Selected Rural and Urban Sites in Ethiopia.* FSS Discussion Paper No. 3. Addis Ababa: Forum for Social Studies.

CSO/A (Central Statistical Office/Authority) 1987. Time Series Data on Area, Production and Yield of Major Crops 1979/80 - 1985/86. Addis Ababa, October.

_____ 1989. Agricultural Sample Survey 1987/88: Results on Area, Production and Yield of Major Crops. Addis Ababa.

_____ 1990. Agricultural Sample Survey 1988/89. Area, Production and Yield of Major Crops. Addis Ababa.

_____ 1991. The 1984 Population and Housing Census of Ethiopia. Analytical Report. Addis Ababa.

_____ 1993. Report on the National Rural Nutrition Survey, Core Module, March 1992. Addis Ababa, May.

_____ 1995 to 2001. Agricultural Sample Survey [1993/94 - 2001]. Reports on Area, Production and Yield of Major Crops. Addis Ababa.

_____ 1998. Agricultural Sample Survey 1997/98 (1990 E.C). Report on Land Utilization (Private Peasant Holdings) Vol. IV. Addis Ababa, December.

_____ 1999. The 1994 Population and Housing Census of Ethiopia. Results at Country Level, Vol. II Analytical Report. Addis Ababa, June.

_____ 2001. Report on the Year 2000 Welfare Monitoring Survey. Addis Ababa, April.

CSA and ORC Macro 2001. Ethiopia Demographic and Health Survey 2000. Addis Ababa, May.

Dessalegn Rahmato 1986. Moral Crusaders and Incipient Capitalists: Mechanized Agriculture and Its Critics in Ethiopia. In *Proceedings of the Third Annual Seminar of the Department of History*, Addis Ababa University, pp. 69-90.

_____1991. Investing in Tradition. *Sociologia Ruralis*, xxi, 2/3:169-183

_____1994. Neither Feast nor Famine: Prospects for Food Security. In Abebe Zegeye and S. Pausewang (eds), *Ethiopia in Change*, London, British Academic Press, pp. 192-208.

_____ 1995. Peasant Agriculture under the Old Regime. In Shiferaw Bekele (ed) *An Economic History of Ethiopia*, Dakar, CODESRIA Book Series, pp. 143-193.

_____ 1997. Manufacturing Poverty: Rural Policy and Micro-Agriculture. Paper delivered at the IDR workshop on Access to Land, Addis Ababa, November.

DPPC (Disaster Preparedness and Prevention Commission) 1999a. Revised Appeal for Assistance. Emergency Relief Needs in Ethiopia 1999. Addis Ababa, May

_____ 1999b. Climate Shocks, Drought and Disaster Prevention in Ethiopia [Amharic] Paper Prepared for Debate on Climate Shocks and Drought, Addis Ababa, 20 August.

_____ 2000. Food Supply Prospect in 2000. EWS Report, Addis Ababa, January.

_____ 2001. Food Supply Prospect in 2001. EWS Report, Addis Ababa, January.

EEA (Ethiopian Economic Association) 2002. A Research Report on Land Tenure and Agricultural Development in Ethiopia. EEA, Addis Ababa, October

FAO 1985. Food Aid in Figures 1984. FAO, Rome

_____ 1986. Food Aid in Figures 1985. FAO, Rome

_____ 1992. Food Aid in Figures 1991. FAO, Rome

_____ 1995. Food Aid in Figures 1994. FAO, Rome

_____ 1991-2000. www.fao.org

FDRE (Federal Democratic Republic of Ethiopia) 2001. *Rural Development Policies, Strategies and Methods* [Amharic]. Addis Ababa: Ministry of Information

Geertz, Clifford 1993. *Agricultural Involution. The Process of Ecological Change in Indonesia*. Berkeley: University of California Press.

Huffnagel, H.P. 1961. *Agriculture in Ethiopia*. Rome: Food and Agriculture Organization (FAO).

IDS (Institute of Development Studies) 2002. Destitution in the Northeastern Highlands (Amhara Region). Interim Report. Brighton, University of Sussex, November.

Lexander, A. 1968. The Changing Rural Society in Arussiland. Publication No. 7, CADU, Assela, March

McCann, James 1987. *From Poverty to Famine in Northeast Ethiopia: A Rural History*. Philadelphia: Pennsylvania University Press.

_____ 1995. *People of the Plow. An Agricultural History of Ethiopia, 1800-1990*. Madison: University of Wisconsin Press.

Marcos Ezra 1997. Demographic Responses to Ecological Degradation and Food Insecurity. PhD Dissertation, Wageningen University.

MEDAC (Ministry of Development and Economic Cooperation) 1999. Poverty Situation in Ethiopia. Welfare Monitoring Unit, MEDAC, Addis Ababa, March

MOFED (Ministry of Finance and Economic Development) 2002. *Ethiopia: Sustainable Development and Poverty Reduction*. Addis Ababa, May

SCF-UK (Save the Children U.K) 1997. Household Food Economy Analysis. 'Dega' North Wollo, North-East Ethiopia. Unpublished report, SCF, Addis Ababa.

UNICEF upto 2000. *The State of the World's Children*. New York.

Watt, Ian 1988. Regional Patterns of Cereal Production and Consumption. In Zein Ahmed Zein and H. Kloos (eds), *The Ecology of Health and Disease in Ethiopia*, Addis Ababa, Ministry of Health, pp. 94-134.

Webb, P., J.von Braun and Yisehac Yohannes 1992. *Famine in Ethiopia: Policy Implementation of Coping Failure at National and Household Levels*. Report No. 92, IFPRI, Washington, D.C.

World Bank 1996. Ethiopia. Food Security Strategy. Unpublished Report. Washington, D.C.

_____ 1999. Ethiopia: Poverty and Policies for the New Millennium. Report No.19804-ET. Washington, D.C. October

Yared Amare 2002. *Rural Poverty in Ethiopia: Household Case Studies from North Shewa*. FSS Discussion Paper No. 9. Addis Ababa: Forum for Social Studies.

2

Urban Poverty and Urban Governance Institutions

Meheret Ayenew

Introduction

Over the past few years, urban poverty has increasingly become an issue of serious concern among development policy makers and practitioners in Asia, Africa and Latin America. The problem has assumed alarming proportions in many towns and cities of the developing world, and unless mitigated can threaten the survival and stability of urban communities. As a means to reduce poverty, urban governments need to increase access to a wide range of socio-economic services and infrastructure for poor residents.

Since the 1950s, rural development was a priority area of focus to improve living conditions and promote economic growth. The development of cities and towns was not considered important and the possible contribution of urban development to rapid national economic growth was not fully recognized. The rural bias left urban poverty unattended. As national governments continued to look the other way, the plight of urban communities deteriorated and residents became victims of an increasingly severe 'chronic urban poverty' (Meheret, 1999; Hulme, et.al., 2001; Amis, 2002)

The failure of urban governments in providing decent shelter, schools, health services, livable environments, transport, water and sanitation systems, has aggravated urban poverty. In many cases, financial constraints have also crippled capacities of urban governments to meet the growing demand for services and infrastructure. Consequently, the urban poor continues to suffer from widespread material deprivation, lack of economic opportunities, homelessness, and drugs and crime (World Bank, UMP: 1996).

Urban poverty began to capture center stage in the international development agenda starting in the early 1990s. Multi-lateral development organizations, such as the World Bank and the IMF, UN agencies such as the United Nations Development Program (UNDP) and bilateral development organizations started to pay particular attention to urban poverty in response to degenerating social and economic conditions (World Bank, 2000/2001). More and more national governments are currently earmarking resources to develop urban areas and improve living conditions as part of a poverty reduction strategy (Meheret, 2001; WB, UMP, 1996).

Urbanization in the Developing World

For the past three decades, much of the developing world has witnessed unprecedented levels of urbanization with more and more people flocking to urban centers in search of better economic opportunities and improved standards of living. Several inter-related factors, including political instability, civil wars and ethnic conflicts, deteriorating rural economies and living conditions in the countryside, push an increasing number of people to cities. According to available projections, more than half the population of Africa and Asia will live in urban areas by 2020. Already more than three-quarters of the poor in Latin America live in cities and the situation is not very much different in Africa and Asia. Table 2.1 below depicts the magnitude of urbanization in Africa, Asia and Latin America between 2000-2030 (UNCHS, 1996).

Table 2.1: **Projection of Urbanization in the Developing World ----2000-2030 (Percent)**

Continent	Year		
	2000	**2015**	**2030**
Africa	37.9	46.5	56.2
Asia	36.7	44.7	53.4
Latin America	75.3	79.9	83.2
World	47.0	53.4	60.3

Source: UNCHS (Habitat), An Urbanizing World. Global Report on Human Settlements. 1996.

Based on the above table, it is projected that about 3.4 billion people or 50 per cent of the total population of Africa and Asia will live in cities by the year 2020. Such a colossal figure would call for huge investments in infrastructure, shelter, environmental and sanitation programs, provision of clean water, electricity and other essential amenities to prevent widespread poverty. An essential requirement to meet this challenge is the establishment of strong urban governance institutions with adequate financial and management capacity to provide services and facilities. It is, therefore, absolutely necessary that development policy makers reckon the need for establishing strong urban governments as an effective strategy to reduce urban poverty and create stable and prosperous urban communities (UNCHS, 1996).

Urban Poverty in Developing Nations

Unable to cope with the demand for services and faced with severe resource constraints, many cities in developing nations are beleaguered by widespread and fast spreading urban poverty gripping residents. There is now increasing awareness that extensive poverty can engender social and political instability and bring havoc to urban communities. In addition, there is also the admission that urban poverty has become so deep and severe that a coalition of stakeholders is necessary to solve the problem. As a result, most city governments are now keen to create partnerships with different stakeholders and civil society organizations (such as NGOs, community-based organizations (CBOs), the private sector and the poor to fight multi-dimensional poverty afflicting urban populations (Meheret, 2002; UNCHS, 2002; UNDP, 2002).

Chronic urban poverty continues to afflict large numbers of urban residents in cities and towns across Africa, Asia and Latin America. Based on per capita income, one estimate made in 1993 put the number of people considered to be below the 'poverty line' [4] at 328 million or 28 per cent of the total urban population of most developing countries (Devas and Rakodi, 1993). More recent national and urban studies show that a third to a half of a specific nation's urban or city population have incomes too low to allow them to meet basic needs and are thus considered below the poverty line. As can be seen in Table 2.2, for example, a study conducted in 1999 covering 21 sub-Saharan African countries indicated that the proportion of the urban population of 15 countries considered to be below the poverty line ranged from 41 to 59 per cent. Further, national studies in several of the poorest African, Asian and Latin American nations suggest that more than half of the urban populations are below the poverty line (UNCHS, 1996; Elizabeth, 1999).

Table 2.2: **Head-Count Ratio of 21 URBAN SSA Countries Below the Poverty Line (Po)--------1999**

No.	Country	Po (per cent)
1..	South Africa	29.51
2.	Mauritania	30.12
3.	Ghana	30.69
4.	Nigeria	34.72
5.	Senegal	34.94
6.	Cote d'Ivore	37.98
7.	Gambia	40.09
8.	Mali	41.33
9.	Niger	41.60
10.	Kenya	42.52
11.	Guinea	43.52
12.	Burkina Faso	44.16
13.	Uganda	44.84
14.	Madagascar	45.09
15.	Djibouti	45.40
16.	Tanzania	49.58
17.	Central African Republic	49.73
18.	Ethiopia	52.90
19.	Guinea Bissau	52.91
20.	Zambia	53.35
21.	Swaziland	58.58

Source: Elizabeth Woldemariam, *The New Face of Poverty in Africa: Urban Poverty in Sub-Saharan Africa*, Economic Commission for Africa, Addis Ababa, Ethiopia, July, 1999

In sum, urban poverty is exacerbated by the inability of urban governance institutions to provide services and infrastructure to the people. The problem can be mitigated when governments recognize the important contribution of urban development to overall national economic growth and allocate sufficient resources to increase the range of services and infrastructure to the community. It is, therefore, absolutely necessary that

---

[4] Poor people considered to be below the poverty line are those who earn less than U.S. $1 a day.

government policy makers as well as bilateral and multi-lateral aid organizations work together to strengthen urban governance institutions and management capacities for effective urban poverty reduction through the provision of pro-poor services and infrastructure.

Urban Poverty in Ethiopia

The preceding general observation is intended to guide through a discussion of urban poverty in Ethiopia and what needs to be done to ameliorate the problem. In this paper, it will be argued that government neglect of urban development for over three decades has exacerbated urban poverty in the country. The relative neglect of the urban sector has left a legacy of weak urban governance and management structures, poorly staffed and under-financed municipal administrations, obsolete local tariff and revenue structures, critical dearth of trained personnel and crumbling urban infrastructure and services. Such a deplorable organization and management profile hardly lends itself to effective poverty reduction in Ethiopia's towns and cities (Meheret, 2001).

Over the past many years, urban poverty in Ethiopia has been fast growing and measures are urgently needed to avoid an impending crisis in urban life. Its visible manifestations include widespread beggary and prostitution; a growing urban population of homeless and street children; and high youth and adult unemployment. According to official statistics, the level of urban poverty stood at 37 per cent in 2002 and was said to be growing at 5-6 per cent per annum (MoFED, 2002). Out of the estimated total urban population of about 11 million, nearly 4.1 million are said to be leading a life of abject poverty and misery (Meheret, 2001). For some cities, such as Addis Ababa, the poverty figure is a frightening 60 per cent, which would imply that nearly 1.7 million of the city's 2.8 million residents are categorized as below the poverty line and are thus experiencing a life of squalor and deprivation (Abebe, 2000).

In recent years, urban poverty in Ethiopia has been growing at a faster rate than rural poverty. According to available government statistics, the level of urban poverty stood at 37 per cent and rural poverty was registered at 45 per cent in 1999/00. Between 1995/96-1999/00, urban poverty has increased by 11.1 per cent while rural poverty has declined by 4.2 per cent. The data in Table 2.3 provide empirical evidence to the preceding observation.

Table 2.3: **Trends in Absolute Poverty Between Urban and Rural Areas in Ethiopia -----1995/96-1999/00 (percent)**

Location	1995/96	1999/00	Per cent change
Urban	33.3	37.0	11.1
Rural	47.0	45.0	-4.2
Total	45.5	44.2	-2.9

Source: Poverty Profile of Ethiopia, March 2002; MoFED, 2002

Urban poverty has also become a serious issue of concern in most regions of the country. As can be depicted in Table 2.4, urban poverty in Ethiopia has increased in 7 of the country's 11 regions between 1995/96 and 1999/00. The highest percentage increase was recorded for Gambella (57.38 per cent) followed by Dire Dawa (34.55 per cent), Tigray (32.82 per cent), Oromiya (30.07 per cent), Addis Ababa (20.67 per cent), Harar (20.27 per cent) and Somale (15.31 per cent). The evidence presented below attests to the need for a comprehensive national strategy to reduce urban poverty in all of the country's regions.

Table 2.4: **Trends in Urban Poverty Head Count Indices (Po)[5] by Region**

No.	Region	1995/96	1999/00	Per cent age Change in Po
1.	Tigray	0.457	0.607	32.82
2.	Afar	-	0.268	-
3.	Amhara	0.373	0.311	-16.62
4.	Oromiya	0.276	0.359	30.07
5.	Somale	0.016	0.261	15.31
6.	Benshangul-Gumuz	0.345	0.289	-16.23
7.	SNNP	0.459	0.402	-12.42
8.	Gambella	0.244	0.384	57.38
9.	Harari	0.291	0.350	20.27
10.	Addis Ababa	0.300	0.362	20.67
11.	Dire Dawa	0.246	0.331	34.55
12.	Total	0.332	0.369	11.14

Source: FDRE, MoFED, Ethiopia: Sustainable Development and Poverty Reduction. Addis Ababa, Ethiopia, May, 2002

Various studies point to the depth and incidence of urban poverty in Ethiopian cities and towns. For example, a study conducted in 1996 brought out the reality that urban poverty was widespread in seven medium-size secondary cities of Ethiopia (Mekonnen & Bereket, 1996). Much government data and statistics have also proved that the depth, incidence and severity of urban poverty are quite high in most secondary cities. For example, the results of the poverty situation analysis made by the Welfare Monitoring Unit (WMU) of the Ministry of Economic Development and Cooperation (MEDaC) reveal the following poverty profiles for selected secondary cities.

Table 2.5: **Poverty Profile of Five Secondary Cities in Ethiopia, 1995/96 --1999/2000**

No.	City	Absolute poverty level percent of poor people	
		1995/96	1999/00
1	Mekelle	46	43
2	Bahir Dar	38	22
3	Awassa	33	Na
4	Jimma	29	37
5	Nazareth	29	28
6	National	33	37

Source: MEDAC, WMU 1999, MoFED, 2002b.

As can be seen from the Table, the absolute level of poverty has slightly declined for some cities, e.g. Mekelle and Nazareth; and has significantly declined for cities such as Bahir Dar between 1995/96 and 1999/00. On the other hand, the level of poverty has

---

[5] Po measures the number of people (head-count) in the total urban population living below the poverty line.

sharply increased for cities like Jimma. Over all, however, urban poverty at the national level has gone up from 33 per cent to 37 per cent for the period under review.

Contributory Factors to Urban Poverty

Several inter-related factors contribute to fast increasing urban poverty in Ethiopia. In this paper, three factors, viz. fast population growth; unemployment and lack of income; and weak urban governance have been identified as having a decisive influence on the magnitude and extent of urban poverty in the country. The following discussion is provided to demonstrate the link between each of these factors and growing poverty in urban areas of Ethiopia.

Fast Population Growth

High rate of population growth has been a major contributory factor to widespread urban poverty in Ethiopia. Natural growth and rural-urban migration mainly caused by shortages of land faced by a growing surplus rural population in search of employment and better income-earning opportunities are the principal contributory factors to rising urban population. The urban population growth has been fuelled by a number of inter-related natural and man-made factors, including drought and famine, ethnic instability and civil strife, declining agricultural productivity and a general deterioration of rural living standards. These destabilizing factors add to soaring urban populations that place tremendous pressure on municipal governments to provide housing, medical care, education, urban infrastructure, water and electricity supplies, sanitation and environmental protection programs in order to reduce urban poverty in cities and towns across the nation.

Currently, Ethiopia is experiencing a high rate of urbanization that is increasing at the rate of 5-6 per cent per year. According to data obtained from the Central Statistical Authority (CSA), the country's urban population was growing at about 5 per cent per annum between 1995 and 2000. This makes it one of the highest in the developing world. According to the 1994 Population and Housing Census, the growth rate has been much higher for some intermediate towns-Assayita (6.5per cent); Assosa (9.9per cent); and Jijiga (9.1per cent).

In 2001/2002, about 17 per cent of Ethiopia's total population or about 11 million people were living in about 937 cities and towns of different sizes and categories. According to some projections, nearly 30 per cent of Ethiopia's population or about 40 million people will live in urban areas by the year 2020. This is a frightening scenario because it means in less than 20 years the urban population will increase four-fold. The additional population will require an expanded level and quality of all types of urban services and infrastructure in years to come (Meheret, 2001). Table 2.6 is intended to provide data on the projected urban population of Ethiopia from 1994 to 2000.

Table 2.6: **Urban Population Projection for Ethiopia------1994—2020**

No.	Year	Total Population (000's)	Urban Population (000's)	Percent age of Urban Population
1.	1995	56677.1	8681.0	15.3
2.	2000	66755.8	11753.6	17.6
3.	2005	79368.5	15952.8	20.1
4.	2010	94246.0	21400.4	22.7
5.	2015	111583.8	20069.2	26.5
6.	2020	131485.2	39530.1	30.6

Source: Central Statistical Authority, *Statistical Abstract*, 1997. Addis Ababa, Ethiopia.

Unemployment and Lack of Income

According to the GOE's Sustainable Development and Poverty Reduction Paper (PRSP) 2002, the poverty situation in urban areas is exacerbated by unemployment and lack of income. This high degree of urban unemployment was revealed by the lost census which indicated a 22 percent urban unemployment, with the highest rate recorded amongst the youth in the 15-29 age groups. (CSA, 1994). Over the years, this grim reality of lack of employment opportunities has been worsening from year to year as can be depicted by the following trend: the urban unemployment rate which was 7.9 per cent in 1984 grew to 22.0 per cent in 1994 and to 26.4 per cent in 1999-growing by more than three-and-half times in 15 years (Genene, et. al. 2001). Such dire statistics point to the need for significant investment in infrastructure and productive activities to create employment opportunities and income for Ethiopia's growing army of the urban unemployed (PRSP, 2002).

Low income per household can be used as a proxy variable to show the link between poverty and lack of income. According to a survey conducted by the Welfare Monitoring Unit (WMU) of the Ethiopian government, a high percentage of urban households have extremely low incomes per year thus indicating the high incidence and depth of poverty gripping urban families. Table 2.7 provides data on percentage distribution of households by income categories for selected cities in Ethiopia.

Table 2.7: **Percentage Distribution of Households by Income Categories for Selected Cities in Ethiopia--1995/1996**

No.	City	Income in Birr per Household per Annum		
		Less than 2000	2000-12,599	12,600 or more
1.	Mekelle	21.47	69.77	8.77
2.	Bahir Dar	23.44	62.94	13.60
3.	Gondar	30.82	56.21	12.96
4.	Dessie	42.07	52.85	5.08
5.	Jimma	22.57	64.19	13.26
6.	Debre Zeit	26.61	63.82	9.59
7.	Nazraeth	24.94	65.89	9.18
8.	Harar	12.29	66.36	21.34
9.	Addis Ababa	15.69	67.25	17.16
10.	Dire Dawa	15.13	66.60	17.88
11.	Other Urban	30.28	58.67	11.05
	Total	26.53	60.98	12.50

Source: The 1995/96 Household Income and Consumption Expenditure Survey; CSA, 1994.

As can be observed from the Table 7, 26.5 per cent of all households earn less than 2000 Birr or US $233 per annum. Assuming an average household size of about 5 persons, each family member gets 47 dollars per person per year or an average of 13 cents per day. This amount is by far lower than the US $1per day, which the World Bank and other aid agencies use as the income level for measuring the poverty line. From the same table, it can also be observed that only 12.5 per cent of urban households earn 12,600 Birr or more annually (more than 1000 Birr per household monthly). The remaining 61 per cent earn between 2000 and 12000 Birr (US $ 232 - 1396) per year per household. On the other hand, a significant majority of urban households or about 61 per cent earn on the average an annual income of less than 5400 Birr (a monthly income of less 450 Birr or about US $ 52) per household.

Weak Urban Governance

The absence of strong urban governments that can provide adequate services and infrastructure to residents is another important factor that has exacerbated urban poverty. For nearly three decades, the development of strong municipal governments for democratic self-rule and effective service and infrastructure provision has been neglected by successive Ethiopian regimes. The hiatus has left a legacy of weak urban governance institutions and deteriorating urban infrastructure and facilities. These constraints have crippled Ethiopian urban governments and municipalities in fighting poverty (Meheret, 2001).

Urban development in Ethiopia has never received more attention than in the days of the Imperial era. The Imperial Government had undertaken more urban reform measures in the first 15 years of its rule than what the two post-monarchist regimes have done over the past 25 to 30 years. This can be evidenced by the fact that most of the important legislations which govern municipal administration and revenue and budgeting practices today date back to the Imperial Period. The list of imperial reforms includes the following:

- The 1932 decree assigned legal powers and duties to Addis Ababa, empowered the city to provide services and provided for the taxation of urban land;

- Decree No. 1 of 1942 provided for the creation of municipalities with appointed councils under the control of the Ministry of the Interior; it also defined some basic municipal functions and revenue sources;

- Proclamation No.74 of 1945 further elaborated municipal functions and contained provisions for central control over municipalities;

- The Imperial Government issued a series of legal notices and regulations in 1971 pursuant to Proclamation No. 74 of 1945 to refine and update regulations on municipal taxes, fees and dues. Currently, almost all municipalities in

Ethiopia use the 1971 regulations as the principal basis for municipal revenue generation and taxation (Meheret, 2001; Gulyani, 2002)

The Derg brought to a halt most municipal reform initiatives started by the Imperial regime. True to its authoritarian and highly centralized power structure, the military-cum-civilian dictatorship that lasted nearly 17 years (1974-1991) did very little to empower municipal and city governments to function as independent local authorities that can deliver urban services and infrastructure to residents. Indeed, the regime transformed urban governments and municipal administrations into state and party appendages. For example, the government issued Proclamation, No. 206/1981, to strengthen municipalities and UDAs; but this particular step did not make them more autonomous and accountable to the citizenry. The then political environment which was characterized by heavy-handed central surveillance and pervasive control of civil society by coercive state institutions was not conducive for the development of democratic urban governance (Gulyani, et. al, 2002).

The measures that the Derg regime undertook in relation to municipal reform were primarily intended to consolidate and centralize power rather than create self-governing municipal authorities that can be vehicles for democratic self-rule. For example, through Proclamation No.47 of 1975, the Government nationalized urban land and extra houses. This was a stop-gap measure to alleviate the housing shortage in the short run but could never have promoted sustainable urban development. Another Proclamation No. 4 of 1976 was issued to provide for the creation of various levels of Urban Dwellers´ Associations (UDAs). But, these hierarchies of kebele and higher kebele administrations were primarily intended to serve as repressive institutions rather than popular structures of urban governance and service delivery.

After the fall of the Derg regime in 1991, the Transitional Government of Ethiopia (TGE) embarked on a process of decentralization of the country into ethnically-divided Regions. The 1995 Federal constitution envisaged governance structures that should devolve significant resources and responsibilities from the central government to Regional states. A formal goal of the political scheme was to bring government closer to the people through a process of decentralization intended to increase public participation and responsiveness to local needs. There was, however, a major gap in the emerging decentralized political structure with regard to urban governance institutions. Neither the Federal nor the Regional constitutions provided any constitutional arrangement as to how self-governing municipal administrations and urban governments can be created and become an integral component of the evolving federal structure of state and local government. This gap in the decentralization process has not helped in the emergence of strong city governments that can contribute to the creation of autonomous local government for poverty reduction in urban areas (Meheret, 1998).

Apart from the constitutional omission in recognizing municipalities as distinct governance entities, the rural policy bias of the Government has relegated the urban sector and industrial development to a secondary status. The development strategy of the Government is encapsulated in the policy called Agricultural-Led Industrialization-

Development, popularly known as ADLI. According to this policy, the impact of urbanization both in terms of problems and opportunities is secondary to rural development because the latter is the priority area for resource allocation and concerted government action for change and meaningful economic growth. This agrarian focus underestimates the potential of cities and urban centers to be engines of economic growth and effective poverty reduction.

Unlike what ADLI prescribes, however, rural and urban development must be viewed as supportive and complementary to each other. Urban centers serve as market outlets for rural producers and urban areas in turn support the rural economy by providing inputs and technology to raise rural and agricultural production. The rural bias in government policy has produced a situation where cities and towns have failed in their service giving functions and missions. This has aggravated the already poor living conditions of the urban poor in Ethiopian towns and cities. In fact, the focus on agriculture without due concern to urban issues could not solve rural problems let alone support the urban economy. Such inadequate attention to urban issues and the failure to recognize the important role of cities and towns in both national and Regional economies has necessitated the need for comprehensive urban reforms at all levels of government in Ethiopia.

In sum, there has been a long-standing pattern of urban neglect by successive regimes in Ethiopia and this has contributed to urban poverty. One of the consequences of lack of attention to the urban sector has been a legacy of weak municipal governance structures and inadequate management capacity. Some of the consequences of this institutional and organizational deficiency have been poorly trained and demoralized municipal personnel; inadequate finance; weak governance and management capacities; obsolete financial and property management practices; and shortage of essential equipment and machinery for road construction. The discussion that follows will examine a few of the major management and capacity constraints in some detail.

Lack of Trained Municipal Personnel

A competent and well-trained municipal labor force is necessary for efficient service delivery and successful poverty reduction in urban areas. This is an important missing link in urban governance institutions of Ethiopia as can be evidenced by the poor caliber of the vast majority of personnel working in municipal administrations. A survey conducted to assess the management and governance capacities of selected municipalities and towns in Ethiopia reveals the extent of shortage of trained personnel. As can be observed from Table 8, municipal personnel in Ethiopia have a low level of education and lack adequate training to serve urban residents.

Table 2.8 shows that about 30 per cent of employees of the sampled municipalities have an educational level of grades 1 to 8 and about 25 per cent have completed high school. Nearly 55 per cent of the employees have only high school education with no formal training in management or urban service delivery. According to the same table, about 35 per cent have college diplomas and a low 8 per cent have received some kind of college training. Apart from low educational achievement, the vast majority of this labor force is not trained in specific areas and skills of municipal service delivery. It can be generalized that this reality of low educational achievement and lack of management training applies to many municipalities throughout the nation (Meheret, 2001).

Table 2.8: Level of Educational Qualification and Training of Personnel in Selected Municipalities in Ethiopia-2001.

No	Level of Education	Name of Municipalities									
		Assosa	Awassa	Bahir Dar	Dire Dawa	Gam-bella	Goba	Naz-raeth	Shash-emene	Total	per-cent
1	Grade 1-8	5	34	1	583	14	68	193	79	977	30.1
2	" 9-12	8	48	23	548	16	21	102	75	841	25.9
3*	Grade 12-12+2	12	13	4	1105	-	-	23	9	1166	35.9
4	College Degree and above	-	4	2	254	-	-	-	-	260	8.0
	Total	25	99	30	2490	30	89	318	163	3244	100

Source: 1. Meheret Ayenew, *Decentralized Municipal Management in Ethiopia: A Rapid Appraisal of Five Municipalities*. World Bank: Addis Ababa, Ethiopia, September, 2001.

2. WUDB and UDSS/GTZ, Oromia Regional State: Municipalities, Organization and Manpower Study, Addis Ababa, December, 1998.

Note: * Only finance department.

Poor Salaries and Incentives

An additional factor that contributes to the deplorable service record of many municipalities in Ethiopia is the poor motivation and low morale of municipal staff. Municipal employees are paid civil service wages, which are often low and not competitive with the prevailing market rates. This has meant that many municipalities can neither attract nor retain enough trained and motivated personnel to fill badly needed positions, including engineers, sanitation workers, surveys, construction personnel, accountants and managers. Urban residents will continue to suffer from poor services delivery and infrastructure provision unless attractive working conditions and incentive systems are instituted to improve the morale and motivation of municipal employees.

Weak Revenue and Expenditure Capacity

Another manifestation of the consequences of neglect of urban governance institutions is the poor revenue mobilization and weak expenditure capacity of municipalities and towns in Ethiopia. One measure of the weak financial base is low average per capita income and average per capita expenditure. The average per capita income of a municipality is the assumed share of an individual municipal resident from the total revenue collected per year. The average per capita expenditure is the assumed amount of money that a municipality expends for an individual municipal resident. These two measures are often used to assess the financial prowess of municipalities and local governments. Generally, the higher the per capita, the stronger the particular local government or municipality is in terms of finance and thus its capacity to deliver services and infrastructure. A comparison of figures obtained from selected municipalities with data from Africa and transitional economies clearly shows the extent to which municipalities in Ethiopia are weak financially when compared with their counterparts in Africa and elsewhere. Table 2.9 is presented to lend credence to this observation.

Table 2.9: **Comparison of Per capita Revenue and Expenditure of Selected Ethiopian Municipalities with African Countries and Transitional Economies (US $)**

No.	Description	Average per capita income	Average per capita expenditure
1.	Assosa	1.40	1.15
2.	Awassa	4.65	2.88
3.	Bahir Dar	8.82	7.75
4.	Dire Dawa	5.50	3.4
5.	Gambella	2.40	-
6.	Africa	15.20	10.23
7.	Transitional countries	237.00	77.40

Source: Urban Indicators Survey, Habitat, April 1997 and Meheret Ayenew, Decentralized Municipal Management in Ethiopia: A Rapid Appraisal of Five Municipalities. World Bank: Addis Ababa, Ethiopia, September, 2001.

Absence of Government Financial Assistance and Borrowing Authority

At present, municipalities in Ethiopia do not receive any financial assistance or subsidy either from the federal or regional governments[6]. In addition, municipalities do not have borrowing authority to secure loans either from government or private financial institutions. These limitations have exacerbated the financial and budgetary problems of municipalities and thus have crippled their capacities for service delivery and provision of adequate infrastructure. Even more important, the financial crunch has meant that municipalities cannot undertake any capital construction projects or service expansion activities that will require substantial amounts of investment. This state of affairs contributes to declining municipal services and exacerbates urban poverty in Ethiopia's towns and cities.

Current Initiatives in Urban Reform

In recent years, the Government of Ethiopia has taken a number of initiatives aimed at municipal reform. The major thrust of the policy initiative is to provide legal and institutional authority and enhance the management and governance capacity of towns and cities for democratic self-rule and the provision of services to urban residents. The strategy has a number of components, including strengthening the legal identity of cities and towns; capacity building and training in municipal human resource development; capacity building for decentralized urban services delivery (CBDSD); urban revenue collection and administration; financial and budgetary administration; preparation of

---

[6] The only exception in this regard is the transfer of resources to selected big cities such as Bahir Dar and Makalle which have lately received some grant from the Road Fund.

appropriate policy manuals; guidelines and procedures in finance, personnel administration; contract administration and management; property and materials procurement and management (Meheret, 2002).

Regional governments initially undertook most of the municipal reform measures. For example, the Amhara Regional state has taken steps to define the legal status and functions of municipalities. The Region has adopted reform legislation that will create self-governing city and town administrations. Popular elections had already been conducted in 12 municipalities which will soon have independent councils with adequate legal authority to raise revenue and provide services in their jurisdiction. In Tigray, the Regional council has approved a municipal legislation to establish autonomous municipalities throughout the region. All other Regions have also taken or are in the process of undertaking municipal reforms supported by the Urban Development Capacity Building Office of the Ministry of Federal Affairs. At the national level, the Ministry has prepared a 'National Perspective for Urban Development Policy and Strategy' to assist the efforts of the Regional governments in undertaking municipal reforms in the future (Meheret, 2001; 2002).

The sordid reality of urban neglect has rendered the challenges of municipal reform more formidable. The reform process is somewhat complex since efforts to revive the country's municipalities involve a two-step process- legislative re-enactment followed by extensive capacity building and reform. Therefore, it was absolutely necessary to initiate a major municipal reform program that involves multiple dimensions such as streamlining organization and governance of municipalities, management and capacity building, revision of municipal tariffs and rates, training required personnel for service delivery, prudent local financial management and fulfilling the equipment and technology needs of municipalities. The Government hopes to meet some of these challenges with the US$ 26 million obtained from the World Bank through the program called Capacity Building for Decentralized Service Delivery (CBDSD) (Meheret, 2001: Gulyani, et al, 2002).

Conclusion

Ethiopia is one of the fastest urbanizing nations in the developing world. Rapid urban population growth will inevitably call for huge investments in housing, urban infrastructure, water and electricity supplies, sanitation systems and environmental protection programs and programs to alleviate poverty in cities. More important, this challenge will require an adequate municipal management and resource capacity, responsive urban governance and well-trained and motivated personnel in delivering and sustaining services such as water, electricity supplies, local revenue collection and administration, urban planning and sanitation and health areas to meet the ever growing demand for better and more quality services and infrastructure. To meet the challenge, effective government policies to create strong urban governance institutions and management capacities for service delivery and poverty reduction in urban areas are urgently needed.

Fast urban population increase has been accompanied by rising urban poverty in Ethiopia. Some of the manifestations of increasing urban poverty include homelessness, beggary, an increasing number of street children, the HIV-AIDS pandemic and prostitution, all of which are easily observable in the streets of Ethiopian towns and cities. The fast population growth is fuelled by a number of inter-related factors, including natural growth, rural-urban migration of people in search of employment and better income opportunities, drought, famine, declining agricultural productivity and a general deterioration of rural living standards. On top of these push factors, the relative neglect of urban development by successive Ethiopian regimes has contributed to increasing urban poverty in towns and cities.

Urban poverty has reached alarming proportions and unless mitigated can threaten the very fabric and survival of state and society in Ethiopia. According to the GOE's Poverty Reduction Strategy Paper (PRSP), 2000/01-2002/03, the prevalence of urban poverty stood at 33 per cent but was said to be growing at a faster rate than in the rural areas. Urban poverty is so complex and deep-rooted that the Government and municipal administrations need to combine the efforts of many stakeholders in solving the problem. Hence, innovative urban governance arrangements that can foster partnerships among Government, civil society, the private sector, donors and the community are required to effectively fight urban poverty.

An extremely important requirement in reducing urban poverty is the availability of strong urban governance institutions that can cater to the service and infrastructure needs of a growing urban community. These institutions must provide essential socio-economic services, such as housing, urban infrastructure, water and electricity supplies, sanitation and environmental protection programs as a means to reduce poverty. At the same time, they must also generate dynamic economic growth, and create employment and income opportunities to reduce urban poverty in cities and towns across the nation.

References

Abebe Kebede, 2001. 'Poverty in Addis Ababa', ed. Meheret Ayenew, *The Social Dimensions of Poverty*. Forum for Social Studies, Addis Ababa.

Amis, Philip, 2002. *Thinking About Chronic Urban Poverty*. University of Birmingham. School of Public Policy. Chronic Poverty Research Center.

Central Statistical Authority. 1994 Population and Housing Census, Addis Ababa.

Devas, Nick and Rakodi, Carole, eds. 1993. *Managing Fast Growing Cities-New Approaches to Urban Planning and Management in the Developing World*. U.K.: Longman

Elizabeth Woldemariam, 1999. *The New Face of Poverty in Africa: Urban Poverty in Sub-Saharan Africa, Economic Commission for Africa*. Addis Ababa, Ethiopia.

Fenta Mandefro* 1998 *Decentralization in Post Derg Ethiopia: Aspects of Federal Regional Relations*. M.A. Thesis, Regional and Local Development Studies, Addis Ababa University.

Genene Bizuneh, et. al. 2001 *Work Status and Unemployment in Ethiopia. In-depth Analysis from the 1994 Population and Housing Census of Ethiopi*a. Italian Multi-Bi Research Project ETH/92/PO1.

Gulyani, Sumila, et. al 2002. *Municipal Decentralization in Ethiopia: A Rapid Assessment*. Addis Ababa, Ethiopia.

Hulme, David; Moore, Karen; & Shepherd, Andrew, "Chronic Poverty: Meanings and Analytical Frameworks"; Institute of Development Policy and Management, University of Manchester, Manchester, *CPRC Working Paper* 2, 2001.

Meheret Ayenew, 1999. "The City of Addis Ababa: Policy Options for the Governance and Management of a City with Multiple Identity", Addis Ababa: Forum for Social Studies, *FSS Discussion Paper No. 2,*.

2001. Decentralized Municipal Management in Ethiopia: A Rapid Appraisal of Five Municipalities. World Bank: Addis Ababa, Ethiopia.

2002 (ed.) *Poverty and Poverty Policy in Ethiopia*. Forum for Social Studies, Addis Ababa.

1998., "Some Preliminary Observations on Institutional and Administrative Gaps in Ethiopia's Decentralization Processes". Regional and Local Development Studies, Faculty of Business and Economics, Addis Ababa University, *Working Paper No. 1,* Addis Ababa

2002, National Perspective for Urban Development Policy and Strategy. Ministry of Federal Affairs, Urban Development Capacity Building Office, Addis Ababa, 2002.

Ministry of Finance and Economic Development (MoFED), 2002. *Ethiopia: Sustainable Development and Poverty Reduction*. Draft PRSP. Addis Ababa.

UNCHS (Habitat), 1996. *An Urbanizing World*: Global Report on Human Settlements.

2002, "Building Municipal Capacity for Private Sector Participation".

UNDP, 2002. "Public-Private Partnerships for the Urban Environment: Programme Brochure".

World Bank, Urban Management Program (UMP), Policy Programme Options for Urban Poverty Reduction: A Framework for Action at the Municipal Level. Washington, D.C. 1996.

2002, World Development Report: Attacking Poverty, Washington, D.C.: Oxford University Press, 2000/2001.

1998, WUDB and UDSS/GTZ, *Oromia Regional State: Municipalities, Organization and Manpower Study,* Addis Ababa.

3

HIV/AIDS and Poverty

Aklilu Kidanu and Hailom Banteyerga

Introduction

This paper is based on selected previous and on-going community based research by the Miz-Hasab Research Center on HIV/AIDS. These include studies among poor and displaced people focusing on (i) HIV/AIDS related stigma and discrimination,[7] (ii) knowledge and attitude towards HIV/AIDS by internally displaced people (IDPs)[8] and (iii) an in-depth analysis of youth reproductive health based on the Demographic and Health Survey (DHS) Ethiopia 2000.

The findings of these studies suggest that the conditions that contribute to HIV/AIDS infection in Ethiopia revolve mostly, if not exclusively, around poverty. Drought/famine and war/conflicts have impoverished the people and have resulted in large-scale displacement and unemployment that have forced people to engage in risky behaviors that lead to HIV/AIDS infection.[9]

In addition, the findings suggest that misconception on HIV/AIDS transmission and prevention as well as stigma and discrimination towards people living with HIV/AIDS (PLWHAs) are mostly a product of ignorance or lack of information and education that also are more prevalent, relatively at least, among the poor. Similarly, gender inequality, which makes women more vulnerable to HIV infection, is mainly the result of economic deprivation and, hence, the lack of 'power' among women to negotiate sex.

Hence, based on these findings it might be concluded that the poor are at risk and are exposed to HIV infection more than any other group of people. Poor people have less access to information and/or health services and their living conditions force them to practice risky behaviors to meet their daily needs. Poor women engage in commercial sex while poor men leave their families in search of jobs and, in the process, get exposed to HIV/AIDS infection.

Poverty, indeed, is the major driving force behind the fast growth of HIV infection in the country. The Ethiopian people are at high risk of HIV/AIDS infection because the majority are poor, uneducated, and have little access to health services.

---

[7] The title of this on-going study is 'HIV/AIDS Related Stigma and Discrimination in Ethiopia.'

[8] The title of this completed study is 'In-depth Study of the knowledge, Attitude, Behavior and Practice (KABP) of Internally Displaced People (IDP) in Ethiopia Toward HIV/AIDS and their Health Status and Medical Care Assessment.' (Aklilu and Hailom 2002b)

[9] The title of this completed study is 'Youth Reproductive Health in Ethiopia.' (Govindasamay et al 2002)

Poverty, the HIV/AIDS Epidemic and Government Response

With a population of 65 million Ethiopia has the third largest population size in Africa. The average number of children that a woman in reproductive years bears is 6, the infant mortality rate of 9.7, and life expectancy at birth of 52 years. The population is predominantly rural with only 15 percent residing in towns. 44 percent of the population is under the age of 15 and 66 percent is under the age of 19. The population is growing at 2.9 percent per year with the potential to double every 23 years (CSA and ORC Macro 2001).

Poverty

Ethiopia is also among the poorest countries in the world. The gross national product (GNP) is US $100 and gross domestic product (GDP) per capita was US $ 97 in 2000 and has declined to US $ 96 in 2001 [World Bank, 2001]. According to demographic and health survey (DHS, 2000), 75 percent of women and 47 percent of men cannot read. Only 23.5 percent of school age girls and 28 percent of school age boys (age 6-12) attend school. The total share of government budget allocated to health is approximately 5 percent for each year from 1997 to 1999 and 7 percent in 2000. The average real per capita expenditure on health is approximately one US $ 1.30 per person in 2000/1.

Poverty, mostly caused by unpopular government polices and successive droughts, has remained the typical feature of the country for centuries with close to half of the population below the poverty level. In 996, only 8 percent of the total population had access to sanitation and 23 percent to safe water. The absolute poverty status varies from region to region, Tigray being the highest with 57.9 per cent and Harari being the lowest with 29.1 per cent. The national average is 45.5 per cent. [UNDP2 000, MEDaC, 1991].

The HIV/AIDS Epidemic

The first evidence of HIV infection was found in 1984 and the first AIDS case was reported in 1986 [NAC, 2001]. HIV/AIDS prevalence was low in the 1980s, but increased quickly through the 1990s, and rose from an estimated 3.2 percent of the adult population in 1993 to 6.6 percent in 2002 [MOH, 2002].

The HIV prevalence rate among 911 pregnant women is 11.3 percent; with the highest prevalence rate, 12.1 per cent, among younger pregnant women in the age group 15-24. In contrast, the rates are 11 and 7 percent in the age group 25-34 and 35-49, respectively (MOH, 2002).

The current number of HIV positive people in the country is 2.8 million with 105,781 cumulative reported cases. The estimated and projected number of AIDS orphans is 1.1 million in 2002, 1,7 million in 2007 and 2.3 million in 2014 (MOH, 2002). The UNAIDS (2002) estimates that there are 990,000 HIV/AIDS orphan children (0-14). Deaths from HIV/AIDS reported till 2001 (adults and children) is 160,000.

The fast growth of HIV/AIDS infection in the country may be attributed many years of poor governance, civil wars/conflicts, drought/famine that have resulted in massive displacements and unemployment and, hence, undermined the cultural values and capacity of the people to tackle social, economic and health problems. To make things worse, the country has poorly developed infrastructure and limited resources. Health coverage is low and HIV/AIDS is spreading at a fast speed causing the death of hundreds of thousands of people mostly young and potentially productive.

The Challenge

Needless to say that the challenges faced to prevent the spread of HIV infection in the country are immense. Some of the major ones are as follows:

- To start with, adequate and reliable evidence of the extent of HIV prevalence in the country is lacking.

- There is severe shortage of HIV testing laboratories as well as counseling services before and after testing.

- Care and support of people living with HIV/AIDS and/or widows and orphans of HIV victims and their families is far from sufficient.

- Programs that target vulnerable populations including commercial sex workers, the unemployed youth, displaced people, street children etc. are totally in adequate.

- Efforts to prevent mother to child transmission of HIV/AIDS, which is considered as one of the major ways of transmission, is almost non-existent.

In addition to these challenges, the knowledge and behavior mismatch in the country show that there is a lot of work to be done to raise the awareness level of the population. According to a report by UNAIDS (2000), a large majority (82 percent) of women in Ethiopia in the age group of 15-24 have heard about HIV/AIDS and know that condom use is one of the prevention methods. However, 61 percent do not know or believe that a healthy looking person could also be infected with HIV/AIDS. Similarly, in spite of the high level of awareness about condom use as a preventive measure, only 37 percent reported condom use in general and only 13 percent use condom at last risky sexual encounter.

The Government Response

Ethiopia, especially in the last 6 years, has attempted to address some of the challenges by introducing HIV/AIDS policies, strategies and programs.

In 1985, the government established a National Task Force on HIV/AIDS. Following that between 1987 and 1989, two medium term prevention and control programs were designed and implemented focusing on IEC, condom promotion, surveillance, patient care and HIV screening laboratories at different health service delivery posts.

In 1988, the government issued the National HIV/AIDS Policy which focused on creating a favorable environment and a comprehensive approach to prevent and control HIV/AIDS (FDRE, 1998). In year 2000, the National HIV/AIDS Council (which has since become HIV/AIDS Mitigation and Control Office, HAMCO) was established with the objective of overseeing and evaluating the implementation of federal and regional HIV/AIDS policies and programs. The Council has also issued a five-year (2001-2005) strategic framework for the national response to HIV/AIDS in Ethiopia (NAC, 2001) as well as HIV/AIDS drug policy which aims at making retroviral drugs available in the country at affordable prices.

The Council has registered some progress in its capacity as the coordinating body of HIV/AIDS programs in the country. I t has stretched its structure and allocated funds to regional, wereda and kebele levels of government. It has approved 31 projects worth 5 million Birr submitted by non-governmental organizations and focused on HIV/AIDS prevention as well as on care and support for people living with HIV/AIDS.

However, the Council has had numerous shortcomings that slowed down the effort to implement the programs and strategies outlined in the five-year strategic framework. First, the Council, for one reason or another, was unable to utilize the modest financial resources available to it. Second, involvement and participation of the Council at the community level were minimal. Third, co-ordination and integration across sectors were not adequately established. The Council, in general, lacked the capacity and leadership required to face up to the challenges of HIV prevention and care for PLWHAs and their families. [10] Hence, the impact of the Council was quite low, particularly compared to the extent of the problem.

The Major Causes of Poverty

The main causes of chronic poverty in the country are ill-advised and inapplicable government polices of the last three governments, including the current one; successive droughts and the resultant famine; and wars and conflicts.

---

[10] The fund allocated to HIV/AIDS for three consecutive years was US $ 63.4 million (Government loan from the World Bank]. However, the annual government expenditures on HIV/AIDS prevention, care, and services was approximately US$ 5 million, which shows the lack of capacity to utilize resources made available according to program.

Government Policies

Ethiopia has seen three radically different state systems in the last four decades, each one introducing its own constitution, flag and national anthem. This has brought about a sense of insecurity and discontinuity that has significantly contributed to its current predicament.

The Imperial Regime

The imperial regime of Ethiopia that lased between 1941 and 1974 legitimized its power and authority on the grounds of divine rights. It was highly centralized and the monarchy and the nobility owned extensive holdings of agricultural; land throughout the country. Most farming peasants did not own the land they tilled and were tenants of the landed aristocracy. For them, tenancy was onerous and exploitative. Not only did they pay rent, usually in kind, for the use of land but also had to render a variety of services including free labor to the landlords (Dessalegn, 1984).

In the latter years of the 1960s and early 1970s, just before the fall of the imperial regime, a good deal of tenant evictions did take place due to the expansion of large-scale mechanized agriculture. In spite of growing discontent and declining political security, the imperial regime refused to reform the land tenure system and eventually, exacerbated by the immediate effects of the 1973-74 drought and famine, lost its grip of power to the Derg in 1974.

The Derg

The *Derg*, a committee of non-commissioned and middle level officials, adopted hard-line Soviet style communist programs. It was a highly centralized one-party state with power concentrated in the hands of one man. Over the 17 years it was in power, the Derg embarked on several policies that proved to be disastrous and directly responsible for the widespread poverty in the country. The land reform of 1975, which dispossessed the landed classes without compensation and abolished tenancy, was well received at the beginning but consequent policies aimed at socialization of agriculture and redistribution of land created tenure insecurity which soured relations between the farmers and the Derg.

In response to the drought of 1984-85, the Derg also embarked on forced settlement and villagization programs that relocated millions of people in areas considered to have better agricultural potentials. These programs, which involved moving peasant households from their traditional localities, was undertaken through coercion and intimidation. Another unpopular policy of the Derg was food requisitioning, in which every peasant had to deliver a quota of grain to the government at prices well below the market price.

Finally, in 1990, in a desperate move, the Derg introduced the concept of mixed economy that attempted to liberalize the economy and allow the participation of the private sector. It was too little too late.

The TGE and FDRE

In 1991, the transitional government of Ethiopia, *the TGE* (later the Federal Democratic Republic of Ethiopia, FDRE) took over power and immediately demobilized half a million Derg soldiers and introduced a policy of administrative decentralization along ethnic lines which led to the formation of ethnic based regional governments.

Furthermore, market liberalization, currency devaluation, and the termination of all state subsidies which were carried out in the mid-1990s have had adverse effects on the livelihoods of many people. In addition, as part of the structural adjustment program, the government undertook a retrenchment program involving lay-offs of a large number of civil servants from all branches of administration.

In 1993, the TGE proclaimed that that land would remain, as previously, under the state ownership and the peasant farmer would continue to hold usufruct rights. Although the TGE's land polices have been slightly improved from before, the sense of tenure insecurity and the resultant adverse effects created by the policies of the Derg remain undiminished.

The immediate results of these policies included large scale unemployment and ethnic conflicts and displacement of large number of people from areas where they lived for many years. All in all, as an indicator of the sum result of these policies, Ethiopia is now best known for its backwardness, chronic drought and famine that have become the major of factors of the impoverishment of its population.

Successive Droughts

Ethiopia is a predominantly agricultural country, whose agricultural performance is highly dependent on and routinely compromised by erratic rainfall. The pressure on agricultural land is high and per capita holdings are small and getting smaller. While the irrigable potential of the country is high (3 million hectares) less than 5 percent of this land is irrigated at present.

It could be argued that drought conditions in Ethiopia are the results, for the most part, of the failed policies, mentioned earlier. The fact that none of the three governments were able to deal with drought conditions in the country, in the absence of international humanitarian assistance, is a testimony in itself.

In any case, severe droughts (and the resultant famines) in Ethiopia took place in 1964-65, 1973-74, 1984-85, 1994 and, most currently, in 2002. In each case, drought resulted in prolonged hunger and malnutrition, migration and massive displacement of people, landlessness and unemployment among the youth, high rates of mortality and morbidity, and the overall unhealthy and dangerous sanitations and living conditions, particularly in urban areas.

It is also important to note that drought was one of few major factors that resulted in the collapse of the two previous two governments. The experience of the country shows that successive governments did very little to deal with drought conditions in the country. The imperial regime, in the 1970s, steadfastly refused to change its polices, particularly its land tenure policy, and eventually succumbed to the force, the Derg, that made drought the driving force behind its rise to power. The Derg, apparently oblivious to the political danger caused by drought, tried to address it a little bit too late and it, too, succumbed to a force much smaller that itself.

Today, drought and HIV/AIDS are the major challenges facing the current government and it remains to be seen how it will deal with them.

Poverty and HIV/AIDS

The attempt here is not to argue that HIV/AIDS is exclusively the problem of the poor. On the contrary, in the absence of preventive measures, we are aware that any body could be infected with HIV/AIDS at any time. However, in this paper, we argue that the poor are at higher risk of HIV/AIDS infection than any other group of people. Based on the above stated previous and on-going research at our Center, we will attempt to establish a link between HIV/AIDS infection and the impoverishing factors of unpopular government polices as well as successive droughts that have resulted in large numbers of displaced and unemployed people whose livelihood patterns force them to engage in risky behaviors that expose them to HIV/AIDS infection.

Poverty, Displacement and HIV/AIDS

Ethiopia's long history is marked with civil wars and conflicts that disrupted the peaceful life of its people. In addition to lack of political stability and peace, the country has been subjected to repeated drought and famine that have forced millions of people to leave their natural habitat and migrate to other parts of the country in search of food, shelter and employment.

The Ministry of Labor and Social affairs (MOLSA, 1997) estimates that there are about 1.7 million internally displaced people (IDP) in Ethiopia. These include demobilized Derg soldiers, victims of drought and conflicts as well as victims of the 1998 border war between Ethiopia and Eritrea. Today hundreds of thousands of IDPs live in scattered sites throughout the country under harsh and risky circumstances exposed to all kinds of diseases, including HIV/AIDS. To site examples, the tens of thousands of IDPs living in camps in Zalambessa (Tigray), Loggia (Afar) and Mesalemia/Kaliti (Addis Ababa) are mostly deportees from Eritrea. Many other IDPs living in sites in Shashemene and Shakiso (Oromiya) Gode (Somali) and Metema (Amhara) are victims ethnic of conflicts and/or droughts who are exposed to social and environmental hazards that expose them to HIV/AIDS infection. All these are, by definition, poor people.

Furthermore, displacement makes people obscure. The social environment they live is unique in that all sorts of people coming from different regions with different cultural and religious background are forced to live in a camp or a shelter. They lack identity and a shared reference for regulating their way of life. And consequently they are exposed to risk behavior and HIV/AIDS infection.

Displacement affects the well being of people irrespective of age and gender. The male heads of families in most cases abandon their households in search of job opportunities. Some also get killed in the wars and conflicts. Men move from place to place in search of jobs and better opportunities, while their wives stay in the camps to look after their children. These situations make them vulnerable to HIV/AIDS.

For most households of displaced people headed by women, the economic impact is obvious. They have no or little access to social services such as education and health. Consequently they are vulnerable to HIV infection. Although HIV/AIDS has been killing indiscriminately, it is becoming apparent that the poor and marginalized sector of the society is most vulnerable to infection.

Poverty, unemployment and displacement expose people particularly women to risky behaviors such as sex work for income and sex with multiple partners as well as forced sex. Lack of access to education and health services hinders people from being aware and better informed about problems that threaten their very survival, and from acquiring the skills and behavior necessary to help them deal with the problems. As a result the IDP camps, that are symbols of poverty, have become breeding grounds for HIV infection and transmission. Moreover, such places end up as trade centers where people come from all over the country and return home in most instances with the virus. [11]

Poverty, Information and HIV/AIDS

One of the major and intriguing observations in our studies is the lack of relationship between hearing about HIV/AIDS and changing behavior according to information heard. Among the general population, the 2000 Demographic and Health Survey shows that 84.7 percent of women respondents have heard of HIV/AIDS and 72.2 percent believe that there is a way to avoid getting AIDS. Similarly, 95.5 percent of men have heard of HIV/AIDS and 89.5 percent believe that there is away to avoid the infection. However, this knowledge is not transformed into change in risky behaviors. There are four main reasons that might explain this.

First, there is a difference between 'hearing' and 'knowing.' Knowledge of programmatically important ways to avoid HIV/AIDS, particularly among the poor, is low when seen in relation to the epidemic. Programmatically important ways are abstaining from sex, using condoms, and limiting the number of sexual partners. This is a critical point to consider while talking about knowledge of HIV/AIDS and behavioral practices to avoid the infection.

---

[11] The IDP sites in Shakiso (gold mining valleys) attract miners from all over the country who engage with IDP women and thereby infecting and being infected with HIV/AIDS in the process.

Second, in spite of the apparent 'knowledge', there is a lot of misconception about the causes and prevention of HIV/AIDS among the poor and the relatively less educated. In the focus group discussions and in-depth interview conducted in our studies, participants mentioned repeatedly that God has created HIV/AIDS to punish those who are practicing wrong acts such as promiscuity and sex with many partners. The prevailing view among the poor is that it is only the sinner that contracts the disease.

Furthermore, our studies show that people still have wrong conceptions on causes of infection such as eating with PLWHA, touching and shaking hands with PLWHA, kissing, eating raw eggs, raw vegetables and fruits, insect bites (such as mosquito bites), and sharing toilets with PLWHAs. The majority does not make a distinction between being HIV positive and being an AIDS patient. The rumors and gossips are directed towards those full-blown AIDS patients. The disease is not openly discussed in relation to a patient. Other diseases such as TB, pneumonia, and draft are mentioned as causes when someone dies away due to HIV/AIDS.

Third, the failure in changing behavior in spite of knowledge is very much reflected in poverty and the lack of incentive and capacity to change. Although most families would like to live a disciplined life and build a disciplined family, poverty situations have become major obstacles. All informants interviewed agree that living conditions of families mostly headed by women make them vulnerable to the disease. Such women undertake sex work openly or in hiding for additional income to support their families.

Young and displaced women get employed as housemaids, work in bars and hotels and do sex work to supplement their financial needs and thereby expose themselves to HIV infection. In one of the IDP sites studied, for example, 11 percent of the residents derive their income from sex work. The situation is similar in the other sites too. The potential customers which include soldiers, track drivers, merchants, and mobile workers and miners, are poor people too and are equally exposed to the danger. As one key informant put it 'people are informed but some say, 'it is better to die of HIV/AIDS after ten years than die out of starvation now.'

Finally, there is the condition of hopelessness, particularly among poor youth. A majority of the youth of displaced families could not continue its education because families cannot support them with their educational needs. They do menial work and most of them remain unemployed. Out of those who work, the majority, including children, are forced to engage in some sort of income generating activities that expose them to HIV/AIDS. Whatever money they get they use it to defuse their frustrations. Whoever makes money spends it in-group. They practice unsafe sex, take drugs, alcoholic drinks, and chew *chat* as means of entertaining themselves. They do not see any future for them. It is difficult to convince people to change their behavioral practices against HIV/AIDS so long as basic necessities of survival are missing.

Poverty, Stigma and Discrimination and HIV/AIDS

Stigma is an attitude of identifying, labeling or attributing undesirable qualities targeted towards those who are perceived as being 'shamefully different' and deviant from the social ideal. Discrimination is the act of distinction, exclusion, restriction or preference which is based on exclusionary perceptions or structures (e.g. race, beliefs, sexuality, gender). It has the purpose or effect of nullifying or impairing the recognition, enjoyment or exercise by all persons, on an equal footing of all rights and freedoms (UNAIDS, 2000).

Our findings show that the main causes of stigma are poverty, ignorance and morality, and fear of infection and ultimate death. The perpetuators of stigma are religious institutions in that they associate the disease with sin and the anger of God; the media because of their stigmatizing and scaring images and messages; family members due to fear of blame, shame and loss of status in addition due to ignorance and fear of infection. Neighbors and friends are involved in gossiping and defamation of PLWHA; health facilities avoid giving proper health care to suspected HIV positive people and see them as terminal cases in addition to the fear of infection; in schools children of HIV/AIDS parents are insulted and scolded; community based associations; and administrative bodies such as kebeles avoid and distance people suspected of HIV/AIDS.

The outcomes of HIV related stigma and discrimination are damaging in that they directly and negatively impact any preventive interventions. They include secrecy and denial about HIV/AIDS, avoiding diagnosis and/or delaying support seeking. Fear, anxiety, depression, anger up to suicidal attempts and revengeful behavior and resentment towards HIV positive family, household or community members are also some of the outcomes of HIV related stigma and discrimination.

The relationship between poverty and stigma and discrimination is that HIV/AIDS stigma is often layered upon pre-existing stigma concerning socially marginalized and vulnerable groups, the poor for instance. It is true that people living with HIV/AIDS may become implicitly associated with stigmatized behaviors, regardless of their status or how they actually became infected. But, for the most part, our studies show that the underpinning factor of stigma is poverty, for the poor have no way to hide it and avoid gossip and rumor.

Poverty, Care and Support to PLWHA in Ethiopia

Many people in Ethiopia perceive HIV/AIDS as a disease contracted by the immoral, promiscuous, drunkard, and marginalized section of the society. As a result, the transfer of knowledge about giving care and support to PLWHA is almost non-existent. And consequently people do not know what to do with a PLWHA relative. No one knows for sure as to who is PLWHA or not. It is only when someone is showing symptoms of full-blown AIDS that people start to suspect and gossip about a person for being a PLWHA.

PLWHA, in turn, do not generally disclose because of fear of discrimination and isolation. Neighbors may not eat/drink with them, and may gossip about them. They can be stigmatized and considered as promiscuous and immoral. Some families may not support them, for fear of contagion. They separate cooking and drinking utensils causing psychological stress on the HIV positive person. Friends may gossip about them. PLWHA hence hide their status and continue to infect others knowingly or unknowingly. The care and support they receive does not balance with the amount of stigma that they experience.

Some enlightened PLWHA in Ethiopia have formed associations by disclosing their sero-status to the public. The main motive is to find ways of getting support and care, for most of them come from poverty stricken background. However, they are finding HIV/AIDS stigma to be a major hurdle in the fight against HIV/AIDS in Ethiopia

Avoidance of PLWHA, discriminating PLWHA in accessing services such as health services, use of provoking and abusive statements, isolation of PLWHA are the major stigma types followed by denial of illness, causing blame and shame to family. Stigma, by and large, occurs in homes, followed in interaction with neighbors, health facilities and community gatherings. Use of abusive and provoking statements, ignoring a PLWHA by pretending not to have seen him/her, putting a PLWHA in isolation, hinting that someone is a PLWHA, avoiding sharing food and drinks, rooms, denying services, not shaking hands, loosing self image are the major manifestations of stigma.

PLWHA reaction to first hand experience is anger, irritation, self-hatred, hopelessness, worthlessness, frustration, and withdrawal, retreat. Only very few dared to discuss their experience. On the other hand, PLWHA use the following as coping mechanisms to deal with stigmatizing and discriminating experience: discussing disappointing experience with a counselor, friends and relatives; retreating from social participation; going to church and praying; and doing good thing to others such as giving lessons on HIV/AIDS.

Conclusion and Ways Forward

Conclusion

The poor are at risk and are exposed to the infection more than any other group of people. Poor people have less access to information and their living conditions force them not to behave according to information received, if any. Poor people have less access to health delivery services. Poor people are forced to practice risky behaviors to meet their daily needs. Women from poor families practice risky sexual activities, commercial sex, while men leave their families in search for job and in the process get exposed to HIV/AIDS infection.

HIV-related stigma and discrimination are typical features of the poor. Stigma and discrimination get worse with the inability of families to give care and support to an HIV positive member. Stigma manifests itself in relation to shortage of facilities such as toilets, and necessities such as food and clothing resulting in the inability to meet the health needs of the PLWHA family member. It also manifests itself in relation to ignorance, for poor people have less access to education; school dropouts are high among children from poor families. Disclosure of sero-status is also positively related to poverty in that the poor PLWHA disclose their status with the hope of getting support from humanitarian organizations.

The Ethiopian people are at high risk of HIV/AIDS infection in that the majority is poor, uneducated, and the health service delivery system is poor. HIV stigma is an obstacle to prevention in that it discourages disclosure and enhances denial. The lack of care and support for PLWHA in addition to stigma discourages people from making use of available VCT services. Poverty indeed is the major driving force for the fast growth of the infection in the country.

The conditions that make HIV/AIDS infection a strong probability all revolve around poverty. Unemployment, prostitution and internal displacements either due drought or wars/conflicts are features of poor people that have consistently lead to risky behaviors. In addition, misconception on HIV/AIDS transmission, prevention, stigma and discrimination towards PLWHA are results of ignorance or lack of information that also are more prevalent, relatively at least, among the poor.

Ways Forward

Poverty is a fertile ground for HIV/AIDS spread in Ethiopia. People are dictating the behavioral practices of the people. In the absence of tangible activities to alleviate the problems of poverty, the activities on HIV/AIDS prevention will not yield the outcomes expected. Poverty alleviation programs based on realistic economic policies need to be in place.

It is indeed important to continue on raising the awareness of people about the disease and the need to give care and support to PLWHA and orphans whose parents have died due to HIV/AIDS. However, the major struggle is how to reduce the magnitude of poverty in the country within a short time. HIV/ASIDS stigma is associated with poverty. We hear of stigmatizing experience only in poor families and communities. PLWHA coming from poor economic background are disclosing their sero status in order to get material and health care support and consequently experience stigma and discrimination.

Attitudinal change towards sex and sexuality is necessary in the fight against HIV/AIDS. Many societies in Ethiopian do not openly discuss sex and sexuality. These critical issues in reproductive health have remained taboos. The illnesses connected with sexual organs remain hidden. Many families do not discuss about the sexual status of their children, too. Attempts need to be made to change this attitude of hiding important matters related to reproductive health. Expanding sex education by involving the youth and parents as well as community and religious leaders can help bring about attitudinal change. Programs and projects that enhance openness in sex and sexuality issues have to be developed and supported. The big problem in HIV/AIDS prevention is the fact that it is a sexually transmitted disease and people are not ready to discuss sexually related issues openly.

Programs that address youth reproductive health, welfare and employment have to be in place. Designing programs that focus on youth health and opportunity for employment can create a conducive environment for bringing change in behavioral practices. Attempts should be made to fund such programs whether run by government or NGOs.

The long term goal should be to reduce poverty, improve the quality of life of the people, make education, health, social, cultural, political participation accessible to all; ensure employment and create a stable and peaceful society; build on good governance and democracy; and respect human rights. Poor governance leads to conflict, war, and poverty. Military mobilization enhances the spread of HIV/AIDS; the readily available sex services enhance the spread of HIV/AIDS; the displacement of people due to internal or external wars and conflicts, and unemployment enhances the spread of HIV/AIDS.

References

Aklilu Kidanu and Dessalegn Rahmato 2000. *Listening to the Poor*. FSS Discussion Paper No. 3. Forum for Social Studies, Addis Ababa, Ethiopia.

Aklilu Kidanu and Hailom Banteyerga 2002a. *HIV/AIDS Related Stigma and Discrimination in Ethiopia*. (research on progress). Miz-Hasab Research Center, Addis Ababa, Ethiopia, with Laura Nyblede of the International Center for Research on Women (ICRW), Washington, USA.

Aklilu Kidanu and Hailom Banteyerga 2002. *In-depth Knowledge, Attitude, Behavior and Practice (KABP) of Internally Displaced Persons (IDPs)in Ethiopia Toward HIV/AIDS and their Health Status and Medical Care Assessment.* Miz-Hasab Research Center, Addis Ababa, Ethiopia, with Emelia Timpo of UNAIDS, Addis Ababa, Ethiopia.

Baardson, Pernille 1993. *Child Prostitution in Addis Ababa. Survey and Background Report* . Prepared for Redda Barnen. Sewedish Save the Children, May 1993.

Central Statistical Authority (CSA) and ORC Macro 2001. *Ethiopia Demographic Survey, 2000.* CSA, Addis Ababa, Ethiopia and ORC Macro, Calverton, Maryland, USA.

Collins, J/Rau, B. *AIDS in the Context of Development.* [n.d.]

Dessalegn Rahmato 1984 *Agrarian Reforms in Ethiopia*. Uppsala: Scandinavian Institute of African Studies.

Federal Democratic Republic of Ethiopia, FDRE 1998. *Policy on HIV/AIDS.* Addis Ababa, Ethiopia.

Govindasamay, Pav, Aklilu Kidanu and Hailom Banteyerga 2002. *Youth Reproductive Health in Ethiopia.* ORC Macro, Calverton, Maryland USA and Miz-Hasab Research Center, Addis Ababa, Ethiopia.

Ministry of Economic Development and Cooperation, MEDAC 1999. *Poverty Situation in Ethiopia.* Addis Ababa, Ethiopia.

Ministry of Health, MOH 2002. *AIDS in Ethiopia.* Ministry of Health in collaboration with Policy Project. Addis Ababa, Ethiopia.

Ministry of Labor and Social Affairs, MOLSA 1997. *Labor Statistics Annual Bulletin, 1996/7.* Ministry of Labor and Social Affairs, Addis Ababa, Ethiopia.

National AIDS Council, NAC 2001. *Strategic Framework for the National Response to HIV/AIDS in Ethiopia (2001-2005).* National AIDS Council, Addis Ababa, Ethiopia.

UNAIDS 2000. *Protocol for the Identification of Discrimination against People Living with HIV.* UNAIDS, Geneva, Switzerland.

UNAIDS 2002. *AIDS Epidemic Update.* December 2001. Geneva. UNAIDS/WHO

UNDP 1992. *Human Development Report. 1992.* New York.

UNDP 2000. *Human Development Report. 2000.* New York.

World Bank 2001. *World Development Report 200/2001.* New York: Oxford University Press.

Contributors

Dessalegn Rahmato is the manager of FSS. He has written extensively on agrarian problems, food security, environmental policy and poverty.

Meheret Ayenew is a member of the Department of Management and Public Administration, Faculty of Business and Economics, Addis Ababa University. He is also a member of the Management Committee of FSS. He has contributed numerous works on development management, urban governance and administrative decentralization.

Aklilu Kidanu is the manager of Miz-Hasab Research Center and a member of FSS. He has done extensive research on population and development, reproductive health and HIV/AIDS.

FSS PUBLICATIONS LIST

FSS Newsletter

Medrek (Quarterly since 1998. English and Amharic)

FSS Discussion Papers

No. 1.   *Water Resource Development in Ethiopia: Issues of Sustainability and Participation.* Dessalegn Rahmato. June 1999

No. 2.   *The City of Addis Ababa: Policy Options for the Governance and Management of a City with Multiple Identity.* Meheret Ayenew. December 1999

No. 3.   *Listening to the Poor: A Study Based on Selected Rural and Urban Sites in Ethiopia.* Aklilu Kidanu and Dessalegn Rahmato. May 2000

No. 4.   *Small-Scale Irrigation and Household Food Security. A Case Study from Central Ethiopia.* Fuad Adem. February 2001

No. 5.   *Land Redistribution and Female-Headed Households.* By Yigremew Adal. November 2001

No. 6.   *Environmental Impact of Development Policies in Peripheral Areas: The Case of Metekel, Northwest Ethiopia.* Wolde-Selassie Abbute. Forthcoming, 2001

No. 7.   *The Environmental Impact of Small-scale Irrigation: A Case Study.* Fuad Adem. Forthcoming, 2001

No. 8.   *Livelihood Insecurity Among Urban Households in Ethiopia.* Dessalegn Rahmato and Aklilu Kidanu. October 2002

No. 9.   *Rural Poverty in Ethiopia: Household Case Studies from North Shewa.* Yared Amare. December 2002

No.10.   *Rural Lands in Ethiopia: Issues, Evidences and Policy Response.* Tesfaye Teklu. Forthcoming 2003

No.11.   *Poverty and Household Food Security in Ethiopia.* Eshetu Bekele. Forthcoming 2003

FSS Monograph Series

No. 1.   *Survey of the Private Press in Ethiopia: 1991-1999.* Shimelis Bonsa. 2000

No. 2.   *Environmental Change and State Policy in Ethiopia: Lessons from Past Experience.* Dessalegn Rahmato. 2001

FSS Conference Proceedings

1.   *Issues in Rural Development. Proceedings of the Inaugural Workshop of the Forum for Social Studies, 18 September 1998.* Edited by Zenebework Taddesse. 2000

2.   *Development and Public Access to Information in Ethiopia.* Edited by Zenebework Tadesse. 2000

3.   *Environment and Development in Ethiopia.* Edited by Zenebework Tadesse. 2001

4.   *Food Security and Sustainable Livelihoods in Ethiopia.* Edited by Yared Amare. 2001

5.   *Natural Resource Management in Ethiopia.* Edited by Alula Pankhurst. 2001

6.   *Poverty and Poverty Policy in Ethiopia.* Special issue containing the papers of FSS' final conference on poverty held on 8 March 2002

Consultation Papers on Poverty

No. 1. *The Social Dimensions of Poverty*. Papers by Minas Hiruy, Abebe Kebede, and Zenebework Tadesse. Edited by Meheret Ayenew. June 2001

No. 2. *NGOs and Poverty Reduction*. Papers by Fassil W. Mariam, Abowork Haile, Berhanu Geleto, and Jemal Ahmed. Edited by Meheret Ayenew. July 2001

No. 3. *Civil Society Groups and Poverty Reduction*. Papers by Abonesh H. Mariam, Zena Berhanu, and Zewdie Shitie. Edited by Meheret Ayenew. August 2001

No. 4. *Listening to the Poor*. Oral Presentation by Gizachew Haile, Senait Zenawi, Sisay Gessesse and Martha Tadesse. In Amharic. Edited by Meheret Ayenew. November 2001

No.5. *The Private Sector and Poverty Reduction [Amharic]*. Papers by Teshome Kebede, Mullu Solomon and Hailemeskel Abebe. Edited by Meheret Ayenew, November 2001

No.6. *Government, Donors and Poverty Reduction*. Papers by H.E. Ato Mekonnen Manyazewal, William James Smith and Jeroen Verheul. Edited by Meheret Ayenew, February 2002.

No.7. *Poverty and Poverty Policy in Ethiopia*. Edited by Meheret Ayenew, 2002

Books

1. *Ethiopia: The Challenge of Democracy from Below*. Edited by Bahru Zewde and Siegfried Pausewang. Nordic African Institute, Uppsala and the Forum for Social Studies, Addis Ababa. 2002

Special Publications

Thematic Briefings on Natural Resource Management, Enlarged Edition. Edited by Alula Pankhurst. Produced jointly by the Forum for Social Studies and the University of Sussex. January 2001

Some Aspects of Poverty in Ethiopia. Papers by Dessalegn Rahmato, Meheret Ayenew and Aklilu Kidanu. Forthcoming 2003

New Series

• Gender Policy Dialogue Series

No. 1 *Gender and Economic Policy*. Edited by Zenebework Tadesse. March 2003

• Consultation Papers on Environment

No. 1 *Environment and Environmental Change in Ethiopia*. Edited by Gedion Asfaw. Consultation Papers on Environment. March 2003

www.ingramcontent.com/pod-product-compliance
Lightning Source LLC
Chambersburg PA
CBHW080844270326
41929CB00016B/2916